Cover photo: Zucker family standing in front of the house
at 8610 Rhodes Avenue, circa 1950
(Source: Zucker family photo)

Charles Zucker

The Vanishing World of My Chicago Childhood

Growing Up on the South Side, 1945–1960

Copyright © 2025 by Charles Zucker

All rights reserved. No part of this publication in print or in electronic format may be reproduced, stored in a retrieval system, or transmitted in any form or by any means, electronic, mechanical, photocopying, recording, or otherwise without the prior written permission of the publisher.

The scanning, uploading, and distribution of this book without permission is a theft of the author's intellectual property. Thank you for your support of the author's rights.

Editing, design, distribution by Bublish

ISBN: 978-1-647049-71-3 (paperback)
ISBN: 978-1-647049-70-6 (eBook)

Dedicated to the memory of my father, my mother, my brother, and all my childhood pals with whom I grew up

CONTENTS

Foreword ix
Preface xi

Chapter I - Setting the Scene 1
Chapter II - Outdoor Games and Activities 10
Chapter III - Indoor Games and Activities 47
Chapter IV - Two Institutions That Shaped My Youth: Arthur
             Dixon Elementary School and Sinai Congregation 64
Chapter V - Visiting the Relatives and Family Celebrations 76
Chapter VI - Out on the Town, Discovering Girls,
             and a Changing Culture 96
Chapter VII - Adult Social Activities and Relationships
              in Business and the Professions 120
Chapter VIII - The Great Migration, a Changing Neighborhood,
               and the Flight to the Suburbs 133

Conclusion - The Zucker Family in Historical Perspective 143
Epilogue - The US Surgeon General's 2023 Advisory on the
           Healing Effects of Social Connection and Community .. 149
Acknowldgements 153
About the Author 155
Author's Brief Bibliography 157

Foreword

It is always exciting for me to read an autobiography that exhibits many of the parallel experiences that I had while growing up in Chicago in the 1940s and 1950s. Charles Zucker may have grown up during that time while living in a different geographical section of the city, but his life in Chatham on the city's South Side was very similar to the events and emotions I experienced growing up in Rogers Park on Chicago's Far North Side. He was born in the mid-forties while I came into the world in July 1943, in the middle of World War II, but both of us were raised by Jewish families. That is true except for the fact that his life was actually part of a more combined mixed Jewish and non-Jewish parentage. But then one realizes we had very similar experiences in our growing up years that included playing outside in the streets and parks of our neighborhoods, joining friends while playing the common games of those years, from marbles and yo-yos to baseball, basketball, and football, staying outside until dark when we knew that it was time to come inside for dinner or bedtime. We also listened to the same radio programs and, by the 1950s, watched similar television programs, attended public elementary schools, and then it was time for high school. Ironically, Charles and I would attend college at the University of Wisconsin in Madison around the same time, concentrate our studies on history courses (I also became a political science major), and proceed to have our own unique careers. However, back in Chicago, we came from parents who considered extended families very important. (I had a cousins' club that brought all family members together on a monthly basis.) And we were given a strong introduction to the arts by visiting Chicago's numerous world-class museums. In addition, we both spent much time downtown at places like Marshall Fields and the Balaban and Katz movie theaters. But it was going to baseball games at Wrigley Field to see our hero of the fifties and sixties, Mister Cub, Ernie Banks, that really connected our growing-up years in the nation's second-largest city. So, simply put, Charles and I were really "brothers of different mothers" in the ways we experienced those two life-shaping decades, and I am certain the readers of this book will enjoy the author's well-written stories.

Neal Samors
Author of *Memories of Growing Up in Chicago:*
Recalling Life during the 20th Century

PREFACE

> In the modern world we have invented ways of speeding up invention, and people's lives change so fast that a person is born into one kind of world, grows up in another, and by the time his children are growing up, lives in still a different world.[1]
>
> ~Margaret Mead

As I am completing this memoir, I am now only a few months away from reaching my eightieth birthday. An enormous amount of time has passed since my brother, Joe, and I grew up on Chicago's South Side. To say that childhood has changed since then is an understatement. I don't pretend that our childhood was typical of how all children grew up back then, but I do believe it was strikingly different from the way it is now. Playing, of course, is what childhood is all about—or should be about. It seems that nowadays kids are hooked into their electronic entertainment almost constantly. If they are not playing video games on their iPads, they are watching TV. If you believe I am making a value judgment about today's childhood compared to what we experienced, well, I am. But I suppose every generation of

---

[1] Margaret Mead, *People And Places* (Cleveland and New York: The World Publishing Company, 1959), p. 304.

grandparents believes their childhood was better than that of their grandchildren. The reason I am writing this is that I believe the type of childhood I experienced is rapidly vanishing.

This story begins with my birth on April 27, 1945, at Ravenswood Hospital in Chicago and ends when we moved from the South Side to Lincolnwood, a northern suburb of Chicago, in 1960. With the Zucker family's move to the suburbs, my life changed dramatically. Perhaps I will tell that part of my life's history at a later date, but for now, I am sticking to the first fifteen years.

In researching and writing this book, I have come to realize how the passage of time dulls one's memory. There isn't any way absent a time machine that I can accurately recreate my childhood for the reader. Yet, with all the limitations of the passage of many decades, I feel it is worth the effort. As Margaret Mead observed, the astoundingly rapid change we experience in modern society means my childhood will soon be a historic relic of a bygone era. I feel such relics are worth preserving, if only to show future generations how we once lived. I hope my efforts will encourage others to write about their childhoods as well.

CHAPTER 1
Setting the Scene

My Earliest Memories: The House at 8610 Rhodes Avenue

Of course, I do not remember the day I was brought into this world at Ravenswood Hospital on Chicago's North Side. But my mother, Leah, often recounted the story for me during my childhood. She was a native of northern Wisconsin who was raised in Antigo, a town of about ten thousand souls located about 280 miles north of Chicago. After my grandfather, Noah Pride, was injured in a train wreck (he was the engineer), the family fell into semi-poverty. My mother was a brilliant woman who should have gone on to college, but like a lot of women from her generation, she could not afford to. After graduating from Antigo High School in 1925, she moved to Chicago to become a registered nurse. The 1930 United States federal census shows that she was employed as a "private nurse," living with two roommates on Lincoln Avenue. At some point, she landed a job at Ravenswood Hospital on Chicago's North Side. She was always extremely proud of her employment there, and, in fact, it became a family joke that my mother would engage strangers in conversation in order to tell them she had been a nurse at Ravenswood. She met my father, Irving, who grew up in Chicago, on a blind date at Wrigley Field. I often joke that the Cubs must have won that day because soon after, they got married.

According to my mother, I was born on a beautiful clear day, entering the world on April 27, 1945. My mother was thirty-eight years old at the time and my father forty-two. I was the second child. My brother, Joe, was four years older than I. He was born at Ravenswood on May 21, 1941. You may wonder why my mother and father were so old by the time I was born. Although my parents were married in 1935, Joe was not born until six years after they were married. The answer, I believe, has to do with the Great Depression and World War II. A lot of people delayed having children—first because of the economic collapse engendered by the Depression and second because of the immense insecurity caused by the war.

I don't remember my first dwelling place after my parents brought me home from the hospital. What I do know is that it was an apartment somewhere on Chicago's South Side. One of my earliest memories is standing with my parents and brother in front of the lot at 8610 South Rhodes Avenue that my parents had purchased in order to build a new home. The bulldozers had already done their work, and construction was about to begin. Real estate records indicate that the house was built in 1949, so I was probably three or four years old at the time. The late 1940s and 1950s were a time of great prosperity in the United States—especially in the northern states with their heavy manufacturing base. My father had held many occupations as a young man (more about this later), but sometime in the late 1930s or early 1940s, he landed a job selling die-cast metal (zinc and aluminum) for Federated Metals. This was fortuitous because the die-cast industry boomed during WWII, and so he earned a good salary, which continued on after the war's end. (His job also earned him an occupational exemption from the draft.) Thus, he was able to save the money to build the house.

The Vanishing World Of My Chicago Childhood

The house at 8610 Rhodes was to be my home from the time we moved into it almost to the time we departed for the suburbs in 1960. Thanks to modern technology, I can go on the internet to see what it looks like today. Real estate companies today describe it as a "jumbo Georgian" house of about 1,800 square feet with three bedrooms, two and one half baths, and a "vintage fireplace" on an oversize lot. It still is a lovely home today, but, of course, it has been modernized over the decades. I have wonderful memories of my years growing up in this house. Unlike most new homes today with their open concept floor plan, our house was laid out in a traditional manner. There was a formal living room with the vintage fireplace, a formal dining room, a kitchen, a breakfast nook, and a powder room on the first floor. It also had a wonderful screened-in back porch where we spent many delightful hours. The second floor consisted of the master bedroom in the front and two bedrooms toward the back of the house, plus the main bathroom. At some point, another bathroom must have been added because I remember only the powder room and the second-floor bathroom. The basement, which was unfinished, was also an integral part of the home. It was where my mother did the laundry, but it also functioned as a playroom for my brother and me. Among other pursuits, we played hockey (no ice, though), basketball, and baseball and fenced with swords that we got through the mail. It also served as a storage facility during the neighborhood boys' annual snake hunt. The basement also had a small separate room for storing canned fruits and vegetables. We never used it for that, though. Why the house had this room I cannot imagine. It must have been a throwback to an earlier era. The real estate companies' contemporary description of the home also states that it has a "fun" extra lot. When my father purchased the lot for the home, he also bought the lot next door. Over the years, my brother and I would have a great time playing sports on that lot. And it provided a place for my mother, who had a green thumb, to have a vegetable garden. She also tended to the beautiful flowers she planted around the house, including peonies, roses, tulips, and irises. The house also had a two-car garage with access via an alley in the back.

**My mother, Leah, holding me at eight weeks old.
(Source: Zucker family photo)**

**My fourth birthday in front of 8610 Rhodes Avenue.
(Source: Zucker family photo**

The Vanishing World Of My Chicago Childhood

**My brother and I dressed up, early 1950s.
(Source: Zucker family Photo)**

**My mother, father, and I behind our house, March 1958.
(Source: Zucker family photo)**

The Chatham Neighborhood and My Childhood Pals

(I have omitted their last names of my pals as it would be impossible for me to contact those that are still living in order to gain their permission to do so. I use only the first letter of their last names. I have indicated the pals who were brothers.)

Brothers Calvin and Jeff E
Richie E
Georgie M
Danny C
Brothers Tom, Dean and Phil M
Joel T
Brucie W
Patrick D
The "Wayo" M

The Chatham neighborhood into which the Zucker family moved in 1949 is one of seventy-seven community areas in the city of Chicago. The *Encyclopedia of Chicago* provides a good description and history of the area. It is located ten miles south of "the Loop" (downtown Chicago) and is defined by a jagged boundary that lies between 79th and 95th Streets to the north and the south and the Illinois Central Railroad and the Dan Ryan Expressway to the east and west. According to the *Encyclopedia*, Chatham was originally more suitable for duck hunting than for human habitation because the area was swampy. It was known as "Mud Lake" to hunters and as "Hog Swamp" to the farmers who began to settle the western region during the 1860s. Residential expansion and population growth began in earnest in the 1880s. The *Encyclopedia* states that the first permanent European American residents of Chatham were Italian stonemasons who built frame houses in the mid-1880s. The roaring twenties brought both a population boom and a rise in property values to Chatham as new residents of mostly Swedish, Irish, and Hungarian ethnicity moved into numerous new bungalows.

According to the *Encyclopedia*, the population swelled from 9,774 in 1920 to 36,228 by the end of the decade.

Although Chatham always maintained a strong working-class population, its middle class began to grow in the following decades. White-collar workers like my father generally earned more than our working-class neighbors. Very few of the white-collar workers in our neighborhood, though, had college degrees. My father, for example, had only a two-year degree from Tuley High School on Chicago's North Side. This was an era when wages for a factory worker were high enough that the family breadwinner could save sufficient money to buy a house. Chatham's population during the period from its inception through the mid-1950s remained comprised almost exclusively of non-Hispanic white people.

The neighborhood the Zuckers moved into in post–World War II America was already well built up. Our house was one of the last constructed on our side of the street. This was an era, though, when houses were constructed by a builder, either one at a time or in small numbers. So most of the houses in the neighborhood were genuinely different—unlike the huge subdivisions of today, where the homes are constructed en masse and are all basically the same. In fact, my parents would become good friends for many years with our builder. The homes in Chatham were smallish by today's standards. Our redbrick Georgian was one of the larger homes in the neighborhood.

In spite of the fact that our neighborhood was relatively developed, large areas of vacant land remained. These vacant areas were an essential ingredient of the childhood we experienced since they gave us an opportunity to create our own "playgrounds." Across the street to the south of our home was a large vacant area (probably more than three acres) where we constructed one of two neighborhood baseball and football fields. It also provided a good hunting ground for our annual snake roundup. We erected another baseball field on a vacant lot on Vernon Avenue, one block west of Rhodes. Farther west still was a huge vacant lot where, as a child, I chased butterflies with my net. A few blocks to the east was another large open space that contained a small swamp. I remember poling around this swamp on a makeshift raft. Avalon Park was the only real park in the area, but it was more than a mile away from where we lived. Though we often went there, it was not the focus of our childhood activities.

In addition to the vacant lots, the streets themselves were used as playgrounds. Across from our house, we put up a hoop in front of a vacant lot. We played basketball there incessantly, come rain or shine—or snow. In fact, I remember my brother and I shoveling snow off Rhodes Avenue in the early spring so we could shoot some hoops. The streets were also our racetrack. With the help of handy parents, we built our own Soap Box Derby cars. One boy was the driver, and another boy served as a pusher. We raced them up and down. Often, we held demolition derbies where the goal was to demolish the other kid's car.

The streets also served as the venue for a game called kick the can, a version of hide-and-go-seek. The playground at Dixon Elementary School, which my brother and I both attended, was where we played fast-pitch: a game in which one boy was the batter and the other the pitcher. There were no fielders. The pitcher hoped to strike the batter out. If the batter hit the ball, the pitcher tried to catch it. A ball hit over the pitcher's head was a single; if it hit the fence bordering the school, then it was a double. A home run had to carry over the fence. Finally, the neighborhood homes and lots themselves functioned as playgrounds. In the summer after it grew dark, we would often play hide-and-go-seek using bushes, shrubs, trees, and anything else we could find to hide from the kid who was "it." And imaginary war games were a mainstay of our outdoor activities as we battled the Germans or the Japanese. In a way, the whole neighborhood was one big playground.

The years following World War II gave rise to the baby boomers, the generation that technically was born between 1946 and 1964. I guess that since I was born in 1945, I would have to classify myself as a "pre-boomer," but I have always felt myself to be a part of that generation. Our neighborhood was crawling with kids. To be sure, older people whose children had flown the coop occupied some of the homes in the neighborhood, but parents and their children lived in most of them. If my memory serves, most families had only a few kids. Maybe some parents—like mine—had delayed having children because of the Depression and WWII, or perhaps it was a matter of choice. But we also had many Catholic families in the neighborhood that tended to push up the average.

The ten friends or so with whom I would pal around during my years growing up on the South Side were scattered for a few blocks around our home on Rhodes Avenue. On Vernon Avenue just to the west of us lived Calvin, who was my age and my closest friend. His brother, Jeff, was my brother Joe's age. They were also friends. Their father, George E. worked for the telephone company. His wife, Deborah, was good friends with my mother. They were of Dutch ancestry. Down the street from the them lived Danny C. His father worked for a successful corporation engaged in the manufacture and sale of truck trailers. They were Italian. Across the street from the Danny lived Richie E. His family, if memory serves, were from somewhere in Scandinavia. Tom, Dean and Phil M were brothers who lived north of Calvin and Jeff on Vernon Avenue. They were Irish. Tom was a little older than my brother, Dean was a little bit younger than my brother Joe, and Phil was my age. Their father held several jobs while we lived on the South Side, but the one I remember best was as a police officer for the city of Chicago. Tom would remain a lifelong friend with my brother. Across the street from us lived Brucie W. I remember him as being quite small. In fact, he played in the Little League at the same time I did and drew a lot of walks because of his diminutive size. His family —like us—were Jewish. I am not sure, but I think his father attorney. Joel T. lived next door to Brucie's family. Joel's father owned a nightclub. They were Italian. Finally, next door to me lived Patrick D. with his mother and a sister. They were Irish. I am not sure exactly where the "Wayo" lived but I believe he was Irish. `

CHAPTER II
Outdoor Games and Activities

Sixteen-Inch Softball: A Chicago Tradition

Although I was just a little past my infancy when we first moved into the house on Rhodes Avenue, within a few years, I was playing the wide variety of sports that occupied so much of my time and my brother's. With the exception of Little League baseball, these were all sports that we organized and played ourselves.

The baseball game we played most often employed a sixteen-inch softball. According to the *Encyclopedia of Chicago,* softball was invented in Chicago on November 24, 1887, by George Hancock, who used a boxing glove to craft the original sphere and a broom handle as a bat. The exact dimensions of the first ball remain unknown. We do know that a fourteen-inch ball was used in 1933 when 70,000 people viewed the game at the first major tournament held at the Century of Progress Exposition, the Second World's Fair

Eventually, the twelve-inch fast-pitch ball became the national standard, but Chicagoans embraced the softer slow-pitch sixteen-inch ball. The fact that the sixteen-inch ball is somewhat softer than its twelve-inch cousin allows the sixteen-inch game to be played barehanded. This means it's less expensive to play because you do not have to fork out a lot of money for a glove. This fact undoubtedly helped spread the popularity of the game among lower-income Chicagoans.

The downside of playing barehanded is that the sixteen-inch softball isn't that soft when it comes out of the box. In fact, it is quite hard. I always joked that you could tell when a man was from Chicago because he would have one or more bent fingers on his hands—me included. You can go online and watch entertaining videos about the sport today—including interviews with surgeons whose job it is to repair badly mangled fingers. A line drive with a new ball when you were playing third base wasn't any fun. My brother often played third and remembered with horror the shots hit his way with rock-hard balls fresh out of the box. Sixteen-inch softball remains an incredibly popular sport in Chicagoland today with numerous leagues and even a Hall of Fame that opened in 2014.

The sixteen-inch Clincher softballs we purchased back in the 1950s cost around three or four dollars. Today, you can buy them online for as little as fifteen dollars. But if you wish to purchase Wilson's Windy City model made of genuine leather, it will set you back about one hundred and sixty bucks. I still remember taking a new Clincher out of its box at the softball field the kids had constructed in the big vacant lot on Vernon Avenue with a mixture of excitement and dread: excitement because we were going to play with a brand-new ball and dread because I knew how hard the ball would be for the first few innings until it got softened up by some hard line drives or long home runs to left field.

Today, several houses occupy that vacant lot, which was actually two or three lots, bordered on the east by Vernon Avenue and on the south by 86th Street. To hit a home run to left field, you had to hit a monstrous drive over the fielder's head into the alley. By the time the outfielder retrieved the ball, you had already circled the bases. The distance to 86th Street in right field was shorter, but since most of us were right handed, home runs were more often hit to left field.

We chose up sides in the traditional manner of kids playing baseball: the best players got selected early and the weaker players later. Of course, on most occasions, we did not have the full complement of eighteen players required for a full-scale baseball game, so some positions went unoccupied. The pitcher in sixteen-inch softball tosses the ball underhanded to the batter. It's slow pitch, so very few batters struck out. But a clever pitcher could make it harder for a batter to hit the ball squarely by pitching inside or outside or up or down. You could also vary the speed of the pitch to some degree. Sometimes one kid served as the umpire. It's been more than sixty years since I played my last game of sixteen-inch softball on our makeshift baseball field, so I have forgotten some of the details of the games. What I do remember is that they were tremendous fun.

The Basketball Court on Rhodes Avenue

As previously mentioned, sometime after we moved into our house, the kids in the neighborhood with the help of parents built a basketball pole across and slightly down the street from our house. For the entire time we lived on Rhodes Avenue, there was a vacant lot right behind the pole. This meant that we were not playing hoops in someone's front yard. We played pretty much year round, though the long and cold Chicago winters curtailed play pretty much from sometime in November through early March. Much like in our softball games, we chose sides. The first team to score a certain number of points won the game. Of course, we also played endless games of "horse." My brother, who grew to be six feet three inches tall, became a superb basketball player, honing his skills on our homemade court. As a senior at Hirsch High School, he would become one of the top scorers in the city of Chicago. I was a darned good basketball player, too, as a youngster, but as I grew older, my athletic prowess tapered off (sigh). You might ask, "But what about the traffic on Rhodes Avenue?" Well, of course, there was some: perhaps a car every two or three minutes. I don't remember that it interfered with our games much. When one of us did spot a vehicle coming our way, he would holler, "Car coming," and the game would be suspended for a minute or two. The drivers did not seem to mind. It was a pretty kid-friendly community.

Football on Our Other Vacant Lots

Most of our football games were played on the other big vacant lot in the neighborhood—the one to the south of our house and across the street. Most of the time, we played tag football. Three or four kids on each team were all we needed. The team on offense would have a huddle where the quarterback would lay out the play. My brother might say, "Charlie, you go down five yards and cut to the left; Dean, you go long; Calvin, you go down ten yards and cut back to me." One of us would center the ball to the QB, who would drop back to pass. Of course, he also had the option of faking a pass and taking off for a run. The boy on defense whose job it was to cover the QB had to count to five—"One, one thousand; two, one thousand; three, one thousand; four, one thousand; five, one thousand"—before he could rush the QB.

We liked to run trick plays. Our favorite was the Statue of Liberty. According to Wikipedia, the most common variation of this play involves the QB taking the snap from the center, dropping back, and gripping the ball with two hands as if getting ready to pass. He then places the ball behind his back with his non-throwing hand while pretending to toss the ball down the field. Meanwhile, during the fake pass, a wide receiver has circled around behind him to whom the QB hands off the ball. With the defense totally tricked out of position, the wide receiver runs for a big gain. When done correctly, the QB's pose resembles that of the Statue of Liberty. God knows how many times we ran that one over the years. You would have thought the defensive team would have seen it coming after so many attempts, but it often worked. Wikipedia documents a number of occasions on which this play (or variants of it) have been successfully employed in both college and professional games. We also played tackle football. I know I had shoulder pads and a helmet, but to the best of my memory, we played relatively few games. Maybe this was because Pop Warner football was not officially incorporated until 1959.

Golfing in the Fields and Beyond

Unlike kids nowadays, who often begin taking golf lessons from pros at the tender age of seven or eight, we learned how to play golf by whacking golf balls around in our vacant lots. I am sure there were kids on the South Side of Chicago who took golf lessons. Perhaps their parents belonged to the famous Midlothian Country Club far to the south of Chatham. But, at the time, the idea that my brother, Joe, or I would take a golf lesson from a pro seemed as unlikely as taking a lesson from an alien on how to pilot a flying saucer. Though my dad liked to play golf, he did not play that often. He did own a set of clubs that must have been twenty or thirty years old at the time. Brother Joe and I used them to practice hitting golf balls that had been hacked around a lot. Most of them had big cuts in their covers.

I am not certain how I learned to swing a golf club. Golf was becoming extremely popular in the 1950s. Ben Hogan and Slammin' Sammy Snead had both become big celebrities. Possibly, my brother and I watched some early golf contests on our black-and-white TV. The first Masters Tournament to be televised was in 1956. Jack Burke Jr., won and took home the first prize money of $6,000.

Eventually, of course, we ventured out onto one of Chicago's many public courses. I don't remember for sure, but the first course I ever played may have been Jackson Park, about five miles from where we lived. It's situated on land that once held the World's Columbian Exposition of 1893; the golf course opened six years later in 1899. Much of my golfing experience while growing up, though, happened after we moved from the South Side to Lincolnwood. I remember going with my father to pick out a set of brand-new clubs and a bag for my sixteenth birthday. I selected a set of Sam Sneed signature Wilson clubs. Woods were still made of wood back then instead of metal. The heads of my driver and fairway clubs were constructed out of beautiful persimmon. Even though we had moved to the North Side, my brother and I still often played golf with one or more of the M brothers from the old neighborhood. We played on Cook County Forest Preserve courses—most often the eighteen-hole Edgebrook layout, but also at the nine-hole Caldwell course. In those days, there was no pre-selection of tee times on these courses. It was first come, first served.

I have a bone to pick with people who think that golf is a game only for the rich. Golfers from all different social and economic classes arose early in the mornings on the weekend to tee off at the Forest Preserve courses. I remember arriving at Edgebrook with my brother by seven a.m. on a Saturday only to find twenty or thirty golfers ahead of us. We teed off from rubber mats. Both Edgebrook and Caldwell were (and probably still are) like shooting galleries, with fairways for many holes not separated by trees or anything else. Balls flew all over the place. You were lucky to finish a round without getting clocked by an errant shot. The fairways and greens hardly looked like Augusta National. Still, it was great fun.

Our golfing experiences were not limited to playing regulation golf courses. My brother and I played on some of the miniature golf courses that were springing up around Chicago, but my fondest recollections are of playing on the miniature golf courses we built ourselves in the neighborhood's vacant lots. I wish I had a diagram or a photograph of one those courses, but I don't. We had all sorts of tough trick holes—some with ramps we constructed out of wood.

Playing with Marbles: A Nearly Extinct Sport

Many of our sports activities could be played either outdoors or indoors. In the 1950s, we spent many happy hours playing with marbles. When the weather was nice, we played marbles outside, but during much of the year, we played inside. You might argue that playing marbles does not exactly qualify as a sporting activity, but it has all the elements of a sports event—except perhaps physical activity. Here's how to play marbles in case you do not know. If you're outside, you can draw a circle in the dirt, perhaps five feet in diameter; if you are inside, you can make a circle with a string. Inside the circle, the players set up thirteen marbles diagonally. Players take turns with their "shooters" (larger marbles), trying to knock one or more of the smaller ones (also called mibs) out of the ring. The shooter's hands and feet must remain outside the circle at all times, or a foul will be declared. But the shooter can shoot from any position outside the ring. If you knock a mib out of the ring, you get to take another turn; you lose your turn when you fail to knock a mib out of the ring. The game ends when all the mibs have been knocked out of the ring. The player with the most marbles is declared the winner.

The game can be played for "funsies," meaning the marbles are returned to the original owners at the end of the game, or for "keepsies," meaning each player retains the ones they knocked out of the circle. Sometimes players used "steelies"—steel ball bearings—as their shooters, but all the players had to agree to this. In my day, games that were played for keepsies were often quite intense. I remember many a marble player going home heartbroken because they had lost some of their most prized marbles. On occasion, that player was me (sob, sob). The players were heartbroken because the most prized marbles were quite beautiful. Though originally made out of clay and stone in ancient times, most of the marbles we played with were made out of glass. Machine-made glass marbles began to be manufactured in Ohio early in the twentieth century and dominated the world market by the 1920s. Some of our marbles were also made out of agate. Today, there's a lively market for the most beautiful and rare marbles—some have sold for over $10,000 at auction.

What happened to marbles? Today, although there's still a national marbles tournament for youngsters, the game has become nearly extinct. An article by Matthew Wills entitled "Losing Our Marbles" published in JSTOR Daily (June 25, 2018) discusses the decline of the game. Wills cites a publication by retired geography professor Malcolm Comeaux bemoaning the decline of marbles ("'Caniques': Marbles and Marble Games as Played in South Louisiana at Mid-Twentieth Century," *The Journal of the Louisiana Historical Association* 52, No 3, Summer 2011). Comeaux, who was born in 1938, played marbles until 1952. The last time he saw kids playing was in 1960. His son, born in 1971, never played the game.

My wife and I had a similar experience. Our twin sons, Noah and Sasha, were born in 1976. When they were children, we bought them a bag of beautiful marbles and taught them how to play. They hardly ever touched them. Guess who has the bag of marbles today? Wills notes that marbles were a form of spontaneous and unsupervised play policed by the players themselves. The disappearance of marbles from the games that children play today is symbolic of what happened to the childhood I experienced on the South Side of Chicago. Most of the games we played we organized and supervised ourselves. Today, the availability of endless plastic toys; organized sports like the Little League, Pop Warner football, soccer, and so on; the near addiction of children to electronic games; the virtual end of walking to and from school; the rarity of empty fields in suburbia; and the advent of "helicopter" parents have all contributed to a society that has lost its marbles.

Playing with Yo-Yos: "Walking the Dog" and More

Yo-yos is another popular game from my childhood that has gone into a tailspin. Children still play with yo-yos but not nearly as much as we did. You probably have seen a yo-yo, but in case you have not, it is a toy consisting of an axle connected to two disks and a string looped around the axle, similar to a spool. According to Wikipedia, it's an ancient toy, with proof of its existence documented as far back as 500 BCE. In the seventeenth century, it was called a bandalore. In 1928, Pedro Flores, an immigrant to the United States from the Philippines, was producing yo-yos in Santa Barbara, California. A year later, the entrepreneur David F. Duncan saw Flores captivating a crowd with a few yo-yo tricks. Realizing the potential of the toy, Duncan purchased the whole shebang from Flores. The game increased exponentially in popularity in the following years, owing to Duncan's ability to market the game.

Yo-yo is played by holding the free end of the string, then inserting one finger into a slipknot. The player then uses force to cause the string to unwind, moving the yo-yo down toward the ground rapidly. The force created by the spinning yo-yo then causes it to move rapidly back upward into the player's hand. Of course, rather than trying to figure out how this actually works from my description, it's much better to watch a demonstration online.

If this were all there were to playing with a yo-yo, it would not be much of a game. But the fact is that a champion yo-yo player can do dozens of tricks—some of them incredibly complicated. Here's a list of ten of the most common yo-yo tricks:

(1) The Sleeper
(2) Walk the Dog
(3) Breakaway
(4) Over the Falls
(5) Around the World
(6) Around the Corner
(7) Rock the Baby
(8) Loop the Loop
(9) Flying Saucer
(10) Fast Wind Up

How many of these could I do in my childhood? I think I could do all of them except for Breakaway and Flying Saucer. Of course, it was not just the tricks we learned to do with a yo-yo that attracted us to the game—it was the yo-yos themselves. Our Duncan yo-yos were prized possessions. We lusted after the fancier models—like the ones that had four rhinestones embedded in each side. Did I ever enter a yo-yo contest? No, I was not nearly good enough. But I remember watching a yo-yo contest that was held in our neighborhood. The boy who won the championship did tricks with an ease that was nothing short of amazing.

If you ask most people over sixty-five if they played with a yo-yo as a child, they will almost certainly tell you yes. And chances are they could—like me—do many of the tricks I listed above. Ask a child under twelve today if they have ever played with a yo-yo, and the answer is more than likely going to be no. It's another childhood game that, in the United States, has given way in a world where technology-based games rule. I am happy to report, though, that the game is still popular in other nations. The four-time world champion hails from South Korea. It's worth watching the championship on YouTube. The tricks performed by the best players today are astounding.

Chasing Butterflies

The South Side of Chicago might seem like an unlikely place for a child to chase butterflies, but the fact is they flourished in the numerous vacant fields within a short distance from our house. I am not sure at what age I acquired a butterfly net. I am guessing I must have been around eleven or twelve years old. Several of the kids in the neighborhood also had butterfly nets.

Early on, I would simply admire the beautiful creatures after netting them and then let them go. But somewhere along the way, my interest in butterflies became more serious. I began a butterfly collection. This meant I had to euthanize the unfortunate critters by putting them in a glass jar (also called a killing jar) and then adding a chemical to it. If memory serves, I used chloroform. At some point, my parents purchased a display case for me so I could exhibit the butterflies I had collected. Like so many things from my childhood, all I have left of my butterfly collection are memories—and vague ones at that. How many butterflies did I display? I am guessing a couple of dozen.

I am pretty sure the following butterflies would have been in my collection: monarch, viceroy, black swallowtail, tiger swallowtail, red admiral, cabbage white, orange sulphur, clouded sulphur, morning cloak, and common buckeye. Of course, the member of the order *Lepidoptera* that my fellow butterfly collectors and I prized the most was not a butterfly at all but the exquisite luna moth—a giant creature with a lime-green wings and a white body. We rarely saw luna moths because they mainly appear at night. And I don't believe that any one of us had a luna moth in our collection. Do I regret now that I killed butterflies in order to put together my collection? The answer, of course, is yes.

A wonderful article by Peter Marren published in the *Independent* (August 11, 2015) entitled "Wings of Desire: Why the Hobby of Butterfly Collecting Is Over—It's All About Conservation Now" describes the fascination that previous generations had with collecting butterflies and why the hobby declined. According to Marren, butterfly collecting reached its peak in the years before WWI, when even future prime ministers Neville Chamberlain and Winston Churchill were avid collectors. Rare specimens sold for large amounts of money at Sotheby's and other auction houses. Marren adds that its popularity can also be measured by the number of long-extinct specialist journals, as well as books, that tended to feature "a bearded gentleman in heavy tweeds, lunging toward a fine specimen, net raised in anticipation."[2]

When Marren was a boy growing up in Southern England in the early sixties, butterfly collecting was still popular. He writes that:

> [Y]ou could still jump on your bike with a satchel and net strapped to your back and ride off into butterfly country without a care in the world. Nearly all my earliest memories of butterflies are caught up in those net-waving expeditions in the French and English countryside with my father and younger brother. My rows of wonkily pinned specimens in their cork-lined store-box were, for a few years, my pride and joy. And long after I had given it all up and moved on, butterflies retained their

---

[2] Peter Marren, "Wings of Desire," *Independent Digital News & Media Ltd*, August 11, 2015.

magic. They were the bright, aerial catalysts that turned me into a naturalist and then a conservationist. To be honest, a buddleia bush covered in tortoiseshells and peacocks still makes me go all dewy-eyed.[3]

So, separated by the Atlantic Ocean, Marren and I had basically the same experience as children collecting butterflies. And we both experienced the decline of butterfly collecting for much the same reasons. When Marren and I were children, butterflies were abundant—even in an urban area like the South Side of Chicago. But by the 1970s, that had begun to change. In fact, for a variety of reasons, including pesticides, the destruction of habitats, and global warming, the butterfly population in the United States is in total free fall today. According to an article published in *Science News* (March 4, 2021), "Dramatic Decline in Western Butterfly Populations Linked to Fall Warming," the number of Western butterflies is declining at a rate of 1.6 percent per year. The report looks at more than 450 butterfly species. Perhaps most disheartening is the collapse of the magnificent monarch butterfly population.

My wife and I have personal experience with this tragedy. In 1988, we moved to Austin, Texas. For many years after that, we experienced the wondrous spectacle of thousands of monarchs fluttering through Austin on their way from their winter home in the Mexican highlands to their summer home in Canada—a journey of well over two thousand miles. But then sometime in the 1990s, we noticed we did not see as many as in years before. And by 2020, if we saw a few, it was a cause for celebration. No, they were not taking a different migration path—they were just gone. According to the article in *Science News*, the latest population count for the Western monarch shows a 99.9 percent decline since the 1980s.

---

[3] Marren, " Wings of Desire."

The downside of children no longer collecting butterflies, Marren observes, is that they have lost a connection to nature that our generation had. He grew up to be a famous naturalist who has published a whole host of books. I did not grow up to be a naturalist. But I retained my love of nature in part because of my experiences chasing butterflies through the prairies on the South Side of Chicago. And, of course, I still marvel at their beauty when I see one today.

The Annual Snake Roundup: Garter Snakes Beware!

Each spring, the boys in our neighborhood conducted our annual snake roundup. Why did we hunt snakes? I suppose that the main reason was because it was fun as we had no practical use for them. We kept the ones we caught for a week or two and then returned them to the wild—at least most of them. The vacant fields around our neighborhood provided prime grounds for the snake hunt. Almost without exception, the snakes we pursued were common garter snakes. The snake hunt usually consisted of perhaps six to ten boys and often took place in the spring or early summer. We would fan out across one of the many vacant lots in our neighborhood, turning over rocks, logs, and anything else a snake might be hiding under. Within a matter of a half a day or so, we had caught a bunch of them. I think we kept the captives in boxes with tops on them because we needed something they could not crawl out of. Once we had enough snakes, we returned home with them. Thinking back on this event, I realize now that my mother was quite tolerant. The snakes my brother, Joe, and I caught did not remain outdoors. They were stored in the basement.

Playing Guns ("No Shooting through Bushes")

My life began just as World War II was drawing to a close. On May 8, 1945, only eleven days after I was born, the war in Europe came to an end. As the news of Germany's surrender reached the rest of the world, joyous crowds gathered in the streets to celebrate, clutching newspapers that declared Victory in Europe. Later that year, President Harry Truman announced Japan's surrender and the end of WWII. On September 2, formal surrender documents were signed aboard the USS *Missouri*.

World War II unleashed a torrent of movies and books in the United States, glorifying the heroism of our fighting forces. Indeed, one of my favorite books growing up was *God Is My Co-Pilot* by Robert Lee Scott Jr. Scott was in his early thirties when war broke out between Japan and China. He was considered too old to fly combat missions by the US military. Nonetheless, he eventually convinced General Claire Chennault, the commander of the Flying Tigers, a group of mercenary American fighter pilots who technically were members of the Chinese Air Force, to let him fly with them. Scott became a double ace, shooting down at least ten Japanese fighters.

His most famous escapade was an aerial duel with the infamous Japanese fighter ace "Tokyo Joe" over Japanese-occupied Hong Kong on Independence Day. In the initial moments of their aerial battle, the Japanese ace badly damaged Scott's Tomahawk fighter plane and was on Scott's tail, about to finish him off, when Scott suddenly dropped his flaps, causing his Tomahawk fighter to drastically lose airspeed. Caught by surprise, Tokyo Joe whizzed by Scott's fighter, and the American ace fired his six .50 caliber machine guns point blank at the Japanese fighter. Tokyo Joe's plane burst into flames, spun out of control, and sent him plummeting to his death. Scott himself was forced to crash land. When he didn't return to base after several days, the Flying Tigers had to presume he had been killed in combat. As Chennault began the awful duty of writing a letter to Scott's wife to inform her of his death, a procession entered the compound, carrying the injured Scott. Warner Brothers later turned the book into a film in February 1945. I must have viewed it a half dozen times growing up.

Arguably the most famous American combat hero of World War II, though, was Audie Murphy. Born in Kingston, Texas, in 1925, Murphy was too young to enlist in the military after Pearl Harbor, but his older brother helped him falsify documents to meet the minimum age requirements. Murphy would receive every military combat award for valor available from the US Army, as well as French and Belgian awards for heroism. He is best known for single-handedly holding off a company of German soldiers for an hour at the Colmar Pocket in France in January 1945 and then leading a successful counterattack while wounded and out of ammunition. After the war was over, Murphy embarked on a twenty-one-year acting career. He played himself in the 1955 autobiographical film *To Hell and Back*, based on his 1949 memoir of the same name. Most of his films, though, were Westerns. Alas, in spite of his fame, Murphy did not lead a happy life after the war, suffering today from what today would be called PTSD. He looked for relief in addictive sleeping pills and alcohol. Murphy died in a plane crash in 1971. He was interred in Arlington National Cemetery, where his grave is one of the most visited.

But back to playing "guns." Just about every boy in the neighborhood between the ages of seven and twelve owned a toy rifle that he had perhaps received as a birthday or Christmas present. At some point in the day, a bunch of us would get together and decide we were going to play guns. But before the game could commence, we had to choose up sides: one team was designated as the American soldiers, while the other team became Japanese or German soldiers. I do not remember how we decided which kids would be on what team. Each team had maybe four or five "soldiers." Once the game started, each "platoon" would seek cover, hoping to surprise the other team. Sometimes it would be very clear that one soldier had surprised a soldier on the other team and "shot" him dead to rights. But often, since we were not playing with paintball guns, disputes broke out as to whether a soldier had been hit.

Of course, we also had to set some ground rules before we started in order to make the contest fair. One of the most common rules was "no shooting through bushes." I remember boys (including myself) arguing loudly that they had not been shot because a soldier on the other team had fired at him through some bushes. Eventually, one team would eliminate all the soldiers on the other team and be declared the winner.

I don't have any statistics, but I would bet my bottom dollar that the team of American soldiers won most of the time.

World War II is still glamorized in American culture today. *The Greatest Generation*, a book by newsman Tom Brokaw, is often credited with popularizing the term, which refers to people who came of age during the Second World War. Brokaw's inspiration for the book came from his attendance at the fortieth anniversary of the D-Day invasion of mainland Europe by the Allies. Although this memoir does not cover Vietnam, it is interesting to compare the impact of the two conflicts on American society: WW II had a great unifying effect on society; Vietnam tore it apart.

Playing with Bows and Arrows (But No BB Guns)

My mother never allowed my brother or me to own a BB gun. I attribute this to the fact that she had been a nurse at Ravenswood Hospital, where she probably saw the damage they could cause to children's eyes. But we were allowed to own bows and arrows. My best guess is that I would have been ten or eleven when I received my first bow and arrow from my parents. My brother and I each had not only a bow and several arrows but also a quiver to keep the arrows in and a target. I am sure some of the arrows had suction cups for tips. However, the arrows that I remember were tipped with metal. Most of the boys in the neighborhood also owned bows and arrows. Most of the time, my brother and I would set up our target and practice shooting at it in the lot next to our house. But, of course, that was not very exciting after a while because we wanted to see how far we could shoot an arrow, and also, we liked to aim at other objects besides the target. We shot at a variety of things like trees, et cetera. Of course, what was true for Joe and me was also true for the other boys in the neighborhood. Since adult supervision was sorely lacking when it came to playing with our bows and arrows, stray arrows frequently flew around. One delightful summer evening as the Zucker family was reposing in our screened porch, an arrow came flying through the screen. Fortunately, it did not hit one of us. I don't think we ever figured out which boy the arrow belonged to.

The most dangerous incident occurred when one boy was hit in the forehead with a metal-tipped arrow. My brother and I concurred that the victim was Phil M. It happened very close to our house because we both remember Phil wailing that he had been hit. My memory is the arrow actually being stuck in Phil's forehead, but I doubt that was the case. He was, however, cut and bleeding and hightailed it for home. Fortunately, the injury proved not to be serious. Today, of course, competition archery is quite popular, so archery stores and ranges can be found all over, including several in San Antonio, where my wife and I reside. And children's bow-and-arrow sets can be purchased in stores or online. The funny thing is that I can't remember in the last several decades seeing a kid playing with a bow and arrow. But that may be because it is better supervised now than when I was a child; most of the activity probably takes place in clubs. That's for the best.

Playing Hide-and-Go-Seek and Kick the Can

The game of hide-and-go-seek is still popular among kids today, though perhaps not as popular as when I was growing up. There are many different versions of this game. Our version, which was played outdoors, went like this. One boy would be chosen "it" to start the game. Usually, a tree would be picked as "home base." After some negotiations, "boundaries" would be defined: that is, the boys who were hiding had to stay inside of certain designated areas. The boy who was "it" covered his eyes with his hands at the home base tree and then proceeded to count to ten going "one, one thousand; two, one thousand," et cetera, until he reached the number ten. During this time, the rest of us would scramble to look for a place to hide. Typical places would be behind a bush or tree or maybe behind a garage in the alley. Once the boy who was it had reached the magic number, he could begin looking for the hiders. When he discovered a hider, a mad dash was on: he had to get back to the tree and touch it before the boy he had found reached it and declared himself "safe." The last boy who was discovered was the winner. The first boy who failed to make it back to the tree before the searcher was it for the next game.

A variant of hide-and-go-seek was kick the can. Kick the can was one of those games left over from hard times during the Great Depression. All you needed to play the game was an empty can, which cost nothing—not like the sophisticated electronic gizmos costing several hundred dollars that parents buy for their kids these days. I remember the game being played on 86th Street between Rhodes Avenue and Vernon Avenue, just to the south of our house. A designated kicker would kick the can as far as he could, and then we would all run and hide. The boy who was it had to retrieve the can and then run as fast as he could back to the spot from whence it had been kicked. During this time, the rest of us escaped, finding places to hide. The game from then on was pretty much like hide-and-go-seek. I remember being very excited while playing both these games. They were, simply put, lots of fun.

I can't emphasize enough how tolerant the neighbors were of our children's games like hide-and-go-seek and kick the can. We were often hiding on their property, seeking refuge behind their bushes or trees. When discovered, we raced across their lawns to try to reach home base before the boy who was it got there, screaming as we ran. And, frequently, our games were played after dinner, when it was already starting to get dark. Did neighbors sometimes complain? Yes. I wonder now, though, why people put up with all this noise and commotion. I have not done any scientific survey, but I believe that today, many of our games simply would not be tolerated in most middle-class neighborhoods. My best explanation of why it was tolerated then was because of the baby boom. Many—if not most—of the families in the neighborhood had youngsters who were participants in the mayhem. And, yet, I think there was something else at work. I can't quite put my finger on it, but I believe, overall, the culture back then was somehow more child friendly than it is today.

Kids' Camping and the Boy Scouts

The South Side of Chicago may seem like an unlikely place for children to go camping, but we did. The preferred "campground" was the vacant field where we played softball. It was during summer months that these expeditions into the "wilderness" took place. The Zucker family certainly did not own a tent or any sleeping bags. Perhaps The E family owned a tent. I remember we did have a primitive shelter of some kind that we slept in. Blankets probably served as sleeping bags. We also had flashlights, of course, and matches in order to build our campfire. I am sure the planning for the camping trip took weeks.

Finally, the big day would arrive, and sometime around sundown, we would haul all our camping gear over to the vacant lot. I remember taking several potatoes with us to roast over our campfire for dinner. After sundown, we would gather sticks to use for our fire, and soon, we would be huddled around its cheery flame. Then we would toss our potatoes, covered in aluminum foil, into the fire. What I distinctly remember is that the potatoes never got fully cooked. After an hour or two, we would pull them out of the fire, charred on the outside and raw on the inside, and eat them anyway. Of course, we all proclaimed them to be delicious. Did we ever make it all the way through the night? No. Perhaps we got cold, or we just grew weary of not being at home in our comfortable beds. So, at some point in the evening, we would head for home. Many years later, I would discover the writings of the outdoor humorist Patrick McManus, who was born in 1933 and raised in Sandpoint, Idaho. Many of his articles are about growing up in what was then a remote wilderness area. Some of my favorite McManus stories are about his childhood pals and their adventures—greatly embellished, of course. I think these stories appeal to me because they reflected the nostalgia I feel now for my own time growing up on the South Side of Chicago.

Camping in a vacant lot, though, was not my only childhood outdoor experience of this kind. Somewhere around the age of ten or eleven, I decided to join the Boy Scouts of America. This organization was founded during the Progressive Era in 1910 by a group of men concerned about the decline of traditional male values as more and more people moved from rural America to the cities. Thus, the Boy Scouts from its inception was concerned about character development. All Boy Scouts had to be able to recite the Scout oath:

> On my honor I will do my best to do my duty to God and my country and to obey the Scout Law; to help other people at all times; to keep myself physically strong, mentally awake, and morally straight.

The ideal scout was trustworthy, loyal, helpful, friendly, courteous, kind, obedient, cheerful, thrifty, brave, and clean.

Our Boy Scout pack met every few weeks or so in the basement of a local church. These meetings were pretty dull. Our Boy Scout pack leader, "Pappy," spent much of the time instilling in us the Boy Scout creed. We lined up military style while he lectured to us. In retrospect, these meetings had a decided nationalistic tone to them. It was, after all, the height of the Cold War. We had to be prepared to fight the communist menace both at home and abroad.

Truth be known, I was a pretty lousy Boy Scout. The same kind of problems that haunted my years earlier in kindergarten returned to plague me. In order to advance up the ranks of scouting, one had to master certain skills. Among these was knot tying. I was terrible at this, but finally, after repeated efforts, I tied enough knots successfully to warrant a "promotion." Much to my surprise, at the very next meeting, Pappy, without mentioning my name, used me as an example of the determination that was what Boy Scouting was all about. I remember being very proud at that moment. It was the highlight of my Boy Scouting experience.

Actual expeditions into the wilderness for our pack were few and far between. Chicago was not exactly surrounded by wilderness that we could easily access. I imagine that being a Boy Scout in Minnesota might have been quite different. Our one camping trip was to the

Indiana Sand Dunes, a beautiful expanse of nature located on the shores of Lake Michigan, about fifty miles south of where we lived. My father, who many years later would prove to be extremely generous when it came to paying for my college education, not only through four years at Wisconsin but also much of graduate school at Northwestern University, could also be incredibly cheap. I remember hoping he would purchase a new sleeping bag for me. Instead, we borrowed a sleeping bag I believe was left over from WWII from a relative, John Johnson. To say it was well used would be an understatement. So what I remember most about this Boy Scout outing was freezing to death in my tent.

Our pack's other memorable outing was a weekend expedition at the Naval Station Great Lakes north of Chicago—a gigantic training station for naval personnel. We stayed overnight in the barracks and were introduced to life in the military. I remember very little about this weekend except for one thing. As we went through the chow line, we were told, "Take all you want, but eat all you take." At some point, I discontinued my membership in the Boy Scouts. It just wasn't my cup of tea.

Soap Box Races and Demolition Derbies: The Legend of V-24

Building and racing soap box cars was another passion of the boys in our neighborhood. Our soap box cars, though, were nothing like the fancy ones costing thousands of dollars that you might see in soap box derbies today. They were primitive things constructed by us with lots of help from handy dads. Interestingly, the soap box derby was also another carryover from the Great Depression.

We had one big hurdle to overcome, though, attempting to race soap box cars on the South Side of Chicago: the area is extremely flat. There wasn't a good-size hill to be found within several miles of where we lived. Thus, we could not depend on gravity to power our soap box cars; we had to improvise. The solution we came up with was that one boy would be the pusher and one boy would be the driver. Driving the soap box car was the desired position since being the pusher meant a lot of hard work. Of course, we took turns for the most part.

Before we did any racing, though, we had to build the soap box cars. I wish I had a photo of one of our vehicles, but I don't. The best I can do is to describe what I remember. Sometime during the winter months, construction would begin. Since several boys had plans to race in the spring, the "manufacturing" process took place in the basements or garage workshops of different families. Just like Ferrari, Mercedes, and Red Bull today have companies producing their highly sophisticated racing machines in preparation for the next Formula 1 season, several families in the neighborhood would be hard at work designing and building the soap box cars.

They were fashioned out of lumber and whatever else we could scrounge that would work. There was no cockpit but rather some sort of open-air seat. A two-by-four perhaps four or five feet wide would be attached to the front of the vehicle. The front wheels would then be attached to the two ends of the two-by-four. In order to steer, we used a rope tied to the front two-by-four. Of course, rear wheels would also be attached. The early soap box cars in the neighborhood used wheels from wagons such as the iconic Radio Flyer. However, sometime later, we discovered that wheels from roller skates increased the speed of the vehicles. Brother Joe and I built several soap box cars ourselves, sometimes with the help of neighborhood dads since my father was extremely unhandy. We raced them frequently up and down the streets against four or five competitors. How fast could they go? To my knowledge, no one ever timed them, but my guess is for a race of maybe fifty yards, we might have averaged around five miles per hour.

Our races became so popular that somehow, the management of the 87th Street Speedway, which was only a few miles from our house, found out about them. The management became interested in holding a soap box car race featuring vehicles from our neighborhood. The idea was that during intermission between the stock car and midget races, we would push our soap box cars down the main straightaway. Sadly, for some reason, the plan fell through.

Although the most common activity for our soap box cars was to see who could cross the finish line first, we had another use for them. We held demolition derbies. The idea for these events undoubtedly came from the popular demolition derbies held back in the 1950s. The 87th Street Speedway held lots of these, and they were enormously popular. In fact, they remain popular today.

In a classic demolition derby, perhaps a dozen or so older cars deliberately smash into one another. The goal is to disable the other vehicles so they can no longer run. The last vehicle remaining operational is declared the winner. Our demolition soap box cars were constructed differently than our racing vehicles: they had to be sturdy. Building one was beyond anything my brother and I could manage. Fortunately, George (father of Calvin and Jeff), our neighbor across the alley, was extremely good at all things mechanical. So at some point, we "contracted" him to build what would become the most legendary of all the soap box cars in the neighborhood: V-24.

Our goal was the same as that of the gas-powered vehicles that competed at the 87th Street Speedway: to knock the other cars out of the contest by smashing into and disabling them. V-24 was a giant: much bigger and much heavier than the competition. And it was well armed. What made V-24 particularly formidable was that it had two big four-by-fours attached to the front to be used as battering rams. The tips of the four-by-fours were covered with some sort of malleable iron.

How we got V-24 out of tour neighbor's basement, I don't remember. Maybe we carried the various pieces outside into their backyard before we assembled it. V-24 struck terror into the hearts of the other kids who had demolition soap box cars. We defeated several before the final showdown with the main competition, which came from another formidable soap box car piloted by our neighbor Georgie.

The showdown took place on 86th Street between Vernon and Rhodes Avenues. My brother was the pusher for V-24, and I was the driver. It's a testament to my brother's strength as a teenager that he was able to push the darned thing. Neither my brother nor I could recall who was the pusher for the competition. Although Georgie's vehicle was faster and more maneuverable than V-24, it was no contest. Within ten minutes or so, his vehicle was in ruins. In fact, to this day, I remember him howling with pain as V-24 smashed into his leg. That was the end. Georgie limped home crying. I remember my brother and I thinking we had broken his ankle. But apparently, it was only a bad bruise.

What happened to V-24? I wish I could tell you it resides in a museum for homemade soap box cars somewhere, but it doesn't. At some point, V-24 was "decommissioned" and is lost forever.

**The 87th Street Speedway: A dream come true for the kids in our neighborhood.
(Permission of Stan Kalwasinski Collection)**

We were lucky boys indeed to have an auto race car track located practically in our neighborhood. According to the Chicagoland Auto Racing website, the 87th Street Speedway (also known as Gill Stadium) was constructed in 1948 at 1111 East 87th Street between Cottage Grove and Jeffrey Avenues—no more than about a mile from our home on Rhodes Avenue. The 87th Street Speedway was the birthplace of weekly short stock car racing in the Chicagoland area. Interestingly, the stadium was constructed originally as the home of the all-girl Chicago Cardinals baseball team. But the team would only play there for one season.

The small baseball stadium saw a one-fifth (maybe it was one-quarter) mile dirt track built inside its premises for the purpose of presenting midget auto racing in 1948. On May 23, Gene Hartley won the season-opening twenty-lap feature event. Ray Elliott scored seven victories during the inaugural year and was crowned Gill Stadium champion. I remember watching many midget races with my brother as well as with the other kids from the neighborhood in the 1950s. I can still see the tiny vehicles skidding around the turns and then accelerating as they hit the short straightaway.

But I remember the stock car races better. As the 1948 campaign progressed, hot rod car owner Chuck Scharf and his driver, Eddy Anderson, convinced the track officials to hold an exhibition stock car race during the intermission of a midget race. After several of the exhibitions, the stock cars were ready for their own inaugural race. On Labor Day, September 6, a capacity crowd filled the stadium to watch the first official stock car races. They were a sensational hit. Larry Johnson of Chicago, a midget racer, walked off with the top money in the twenty-five-lap feature event, driving a 1937 Ford to victory.

The stock car driver my brother and I remember best, though, is Bill Van Allen. He was our favorite. And with good reason. An article by Stan Kalwasinski on the Chicagoland Auto Racing website states that Van Allen was "perhaps the most versatile stock car driver to compete on the Chicago area racing scene during a career that lasted more than 20 years."[4] Beginning with his first race at Gill Stadium in 1948 to his last dirt race in 1972, Kalwasinski adds that Van Allen "seemed to have

---

[4] Stan Kalwasinski, "Bill Van Allen," *Chicagoland Auto Racing.com*

a mastery of short track stock car racing."⁵ Van Allen won a heat during that inaugural day of stock car racing at Gill Stadium on Labor Day. I can still see him driving his iconic 1946 Nash with his trademark number 6 emblazoned on its side to victory as a bunch of us kids sat in the stands slurping our snow cones, eating our hot dogs, and drinking our Coca-Colas.

The demolition derbies, though, were our favorites. As I mentioned previously, the classic demolition derby's goal was not to cross the finish line before the other vehicles in the event, but rather to smash into them so they could no longer run. What fun! The drivers were in old jalopies of various makes. In my mind's eye, I can still see the cars crashing into each other and the steam rising from the ones that had been knocked out of the competition. Demolition derbies were very popular in the 1950s, drawing huge crowds at racetracks around the country. They are still popular today.

The 87th Street Speedway closed after the 1956 season. In October of that year, a large sign went up in front of the property reading that it was for sale or lease. I am not sure why the speedway failed. The venue may have simply been too small as auto racing expanded in popularity across the United States. The 87th Street Speedway stands could hold up to about eight thousand fans, and it was frequently packed. Yet there was an intimacy about it that I fear has been lost. We frequently went down to the pits and watched the drivers and the mechanics getting the cars ready for the next race. Racetracks like the 87th Street Speedway may still exist today somewhere in the United States, but I doubt there are many of them.

How did we get to the racetrack? If memory serves, we walked. I don't remember my father dropping us off at the speedway or picking us up after the races were over, though maybe he did. Joe and I would have been going to the 87th Street Speedway from sometime in the early 1950s until it closed after the 1956 season. So, in 1953, let's say, I would

---

⁵ Stan Kalwasinski, "Bill Van Allen," *Chicagoland Auto Racing.com*

have been eight years old and Joe twelve. Kids went places and did things on the South Side of Chicago in the 1950s that kids probably would not do in Chicago today. I don't have any statistics, but Chicago then, of course, was a much less dangerous place than it is today. Yet I do not think that is the whole explanation. Much has been written about today's helicopter parents, who hover over their offspring. I do believe parents then allowed their children to explore the world more on their own than they do today. More about changes in child-rearing practices later.

A League of Their Own: Girls' Softball at Gill Stadium

You may have viewed the classic 1992 sports comedy-drama film *A League of Their Own*, directed by Penny Marshall. Starring Tom Hanks, Geena Davis, and Madonna, it was a huge box office hit. The movie is based on reality. With World War II threatening to shut down Major League Baseball as more and more players were drafted into the military, baseball moguls decided to give women's baseball a whirl. The website of the All-American Girls Professional Baseball League provides a wealth of information about women's baseball. In 1943, Chicago Cubs owner Philip K. Wrigley and several other prominent baseball men organized the league. A twelve-inch softball became the standard, and a new set of rules was adopted to make the game fit women players better. Wrigley attracted hundreds of young women from the United States and Canada to a tryout at Wrigley Field. Of these, 280 were invited to tryouts, and 60 were chosen to become the first women ever to play professional baseball. Four teams were organized, composed of fifteen women each, in Racine and Kenosha, Wisconsin; Rockford, Illinois; and South Bend, Indiana. In addition to their skills on the baseball field, femininity was a high priority. The players were required to attend Helen Rubenstein's evening charm school classes, and each was given a beauty kit. The goal was to make the women as attractive as possible. Special uniforms were designed featuring a one-piece short-skirted tunic—not very practical when sliding into second base. The league's first season in 1943 was more successful than anyone could have imagined: over 178,000 fans attended the games. Baseball executives, the press core, and the fans were all amazed by how well the women played the game.

The AAGPBL, though, was not the only professional women's baseball league in the country. A second league sprang up in the Chicago area. According to an article in Wikipedia, the National Girls Baseball League was founded in 1944 by Emery Parichy, a roofing magnate, and Charles Bidwell, owner of the Chicago Cardinals football team. (Yes, the Arizona Cardinals originally played in Chicago.) The league consisted of six teams that regularly drew over 500,000 fans during its existence between 1944 and 1954. They played at venues all over the Chicagoland area, including Soldier Field and Wrigley Field. Unlike the competing league, the NGBL retained the soft tossing underhand version of the game.

In 1954, Gill Stadium actually was used for its original purpose. During that year, it was home to the Chicago Bluebirds of the NGBL. I don't remember how many Bluebirds games my brother and I attended, but I know we went to several. And it was at Gill Stadium that my brother and I saw arguably the best women's softball player ever: Freda Savona, who played second base for the Queens. Sadly, 1954 was the last year for the NGBL. Although teams and the fan base expanded for several years in both leagues, women's baseball entered a downward spiral in the early 1950s from which it would never recover. The fact that Major League Baseball games began to be televised dealt both leagues a fatal blow. WGN broadcast its first game between the Cubs and White Sox from Wrigley Field on April 16, 1948, and by the mid-1950s, televised games were becoming widespread.

Today, of course, Gill Stadium is long gone. Google Earth shows that much of the land once occupied by the stadium now appears to be a large medical facility. I wonder if any of the people who frequent the building know that auto races and baseball games once took place there.

CHARLES ZUCKER

Organized Sports: The Little League and Pony League

The only organized sports that existed on the South Side of Chicago in the 1950s were Little League and Pony League baseball. Although the origins of Pop Warner football date back to the 1920s, organized football leagues for children had not yet arrived in Chatham-Avalon when I was a child. But Little League and Pony League baseball were popular.

From the time I was nine years old until we moved to the suburbs, I played organized baseball. Our league had a nice baseball stadium, coaches, umpires, and, of course, players. I do not remember the field's location, but I recall that if you were to hit a long home run over the left field wall, the ball would wind up on the tracks of the ICC railroad. As a nine-year-old, my playing skills left a lot to be desired. But as the years progressed and I grew bigger and stronger, my game improved. By the time I was eleven years old, I was a pretty good hurler. And in my final year, I was a star pitcher—a chunky twelve-year-old, in large measure because of my mother's delicious cookies. I had a straight overhand delivery (à la Juan Marichal) and a drop-curve ball I could get over the plate regularly. But I was not the only ace pitcher in the league: my foil was Tommy a lefty with a fastball as good if not better than mine. We hooked up in several duels during my final year in the Little League; the games were always exciting with low scores and lots of strikeouts.

One day when I was scheduled to pitch, my father's uncle, Sam Messinger, who lived in California, was visiting our family. I have a cherished photograph of me in my Orioles uniform standing with Uncle Sam, who was in his eighties at the time. For the first four innings or so, I was cruising along with a comfortable lead, but then something went haywire. I lost my stuff, and the other team started scoring runs. My big lead was gone. Uncle Sam got so nervous he could no longer watch the game. He had to stand behind the bleachers. Somehow I recovered, and we won the game. That year I made our league's all-star team, and we were in the playoffs. I won our first game, but then the Zucker family had a tough decision to make: we were scheduled to leave on our annual summer vacation to northern Wisconsin. What to do? After a lot of discussion, it was decided that we would go on our vacation as planned. Darn, our team lost its next game. I still wonder what would have happened had I been able to pitch that day.

**My uncle Sam Messinger and me before a Little League game, circa 1957.
(Source: Zucker family photo)**

There is no doubt that organized sports have been, overall, a positive experience for generations of kids. My own boys, Noah and Sasha, joined a fencing club when they were about twelve years old. They had a wonderful coach, Vincent Bradford, one of the early great women fencers in the USA. She competed in the women's individual and team foil events at the 1984 Olympics. Both my boys went on to become high-level collegiate fencers. Countless MLB and NFL players started their careers by playing Little League baseball or Pop Warner football. I have had the opportunity to watch boy and girl basketball players being coached here in San Antonio. In terms of fundamentals, they are way ahead of where we were at the same age playing out in the street.

But you may not be surprised that I have a bone to pick with how kids' sports have evolved in recent decades. One thing that troubles me is the excessive amount of money parents seem to spend on sports equipment for their kids. My two San Antonio grandsons briefly played T-ball in an organized league. There were also regular Little League games going on at the same sports complex. I saw dads carrying gigantic, expensive bags on their backs, filled with their kids' baseball gear. Something about this struck me as excessive. After all, how much baseball gear does a nine-year-old kid need? Maybe a bat, a glove, and a few balls? Sammy Sosa, the former star Cubs outfielder, learned to play baseball in the Dominican Republic with a milk carton that he fashioned into a baseball glove. Sam Sneed, one of the greatest golfers of all time, was self-taught, learning the game by playing with "clubs" he fashioned from tree limbs.

The other troubling factor is that not many kids seem to play baseball, football, basketball, or soccer on their own in between organized games. For many parents, schlepping the kids to a game is just another activity. Possibly, the number of neighborhood games has declined because, on average, parents have fewer children today. As I discussed earlier, our neighborhood was crawling with kids. It's hard to have a pick-up baseball game if there are only a few kids in roughly the same age group in the neighborhood.

Misbehaving: Smoking Cigarettes and Playing Pranks on the Neighbors (Or "Boys Will Be Boys")

The neighborhood boys often engaged in mischievous conduct. We thought our pranks were great fun, but I am not sure the people on the receiving end would have agreed. I hasten to add that our pranks were more in line with the shenanigans that American kids have undertaken from time immemorial. For example, I am certain that if outhouses were still around, we would have had great fun tipping them over. Very little if any of what we did amounted to juvenile delinquency.

One of our favorite mischievous pastimes was to find a way to buy a pack of cigarettes. The first step was to come up with the twenty-five cents or so that a pack of Lucky Strikes or Pall Malls cost. Once we had rounded up the money, one of the braver souls among us would volunteer to head over to a local store to purchase the cigarettes. This, of course, involved telling a fib. When the clerk asked whom the cigarettes were for, they would be told "my dad," but under their breath so the clerk would not hear, the volunteer would add, "won't know anything about it." We did this so, technically, we were not telling a lie. This ruse worked sometimes, although on more than one occasion the clerk sent the kid packing.

Was I ever the designated kid to buy the cigarettes? I may have been on one or two occasions. We would then gather in some out-of-the-way place to smoke them. In retrospect, I wonder now why we all thought this was such a big deal. The fact that we were doing something we were not supposed to do definitely made it exciting. And smoking was such a big deal in the 1950s; I am sure we felt that we had entered the adult world, if only for a little while. If you watch documentaries taking place in the 1950s, it is amazing how much men and women smoked. It is a wonder anyone survived.

By the time I had my own children, the culture had changed dramatically. The tobacco industry had been shaken to the core by indisputable evidence that smoking caused lung cancer, as well as a host of other nasty diseases. I smoked cigarettes (as well as a pipe) into my early forties, when I decided to quit. But quitting was not so easy, I discovered. So occasionally, I would purchase a pack and smoke one surreptitiously when my two sons were not around. But, unfortunately, one day, one of my boys discovered a pack hidden beneath some clothing in my dresser. He was horrified. "How could you do this?" he asked, breaking into tears. That was pretty much the end of my smoking habit, though I continued to bum a cigarette or two from colleagues at work. Later on, I saw the humor in the situation. Wasn't it supposed to be the other way around? That is, the dad catching the kid smoking outside behind the garage rather than the kid catching the old man.

Halloween evening was an opportune time for us to pull off our pranks. One of our favorites was to tie a woman's purse to a long piece of rope. When it was dark, we would toss the purse out into the middle of Rhodes Avenue or another nearby street. Eventually, a car would come along. The driver would see the purse in the middle of the street, think some lady had dropped it, stop the car, and get out to retrieve it. When the person bent over to pick up the purse, much to their surprise, it would suddenly be yanked away. Okay, it seems sort of lame now, but to us it was hilarious.

A more disgusting prank involved finding some dog poop, scooping it up, and putting it in a paper bag. We would then place it at a neighbor's front door, light the bag on fire, and ring the doorbell. On more than one occasion, the neighbor would open the door, see the burning bag, and stomp on it with their foot while we watched laughing from a safe distance away.

Neighbors who for some reason had gotten on our wrong side could be targeted at any time during the year. Our next-door neighbor, Mrs. D, had a boyfriend who often irked us. This was because Mrs. D. owned a lot next to her house (much like ours) that we liked to play in—hide and seek, et cetera. If he pulled up in the alley behind their house to park his woody station wagon while we were running around, he would chase us away. We decided we had to seek revenge.

A group of us got together to plan what we would do. I don't remember all the boys who were involved, but I know my brother and I both were. We came up with the idea of constructing a dummy that was supposed to look like the boyfriend. When he pulled up in the alley around dusk, the effigy would be hanging in a nearby tree. As he got out of his car, we planned to light the effigy, which had been soaked in gasoline, on fire. Somehow, my mother got wind of this plot. I don't understand to this day why she did not put a stop to it. Maybe she didn't like Randy, either, though I doubt that was the reason.

In any case, on the night of the prank, she became worried that something would go wrong—maybe one of us would catch fire. So she took a flashlight from our house and went out into the alley to see what was going on. Just as she reached the our neighbor's garage, the boyfriend pulled up and we lit the effigy on fire. It burst into flames as we all disappeared into the night. There was my poor mother standing in front of the fire as he got out of his station wagon. It must have been terribly embarrassing for her, but I don't remember ever asking her about what transpired between them.

You may remember from an earlier discussion how we would have an annual snake roundup. Although most of the snakes were set free after a few days no worse for the experience, some of the boys in the neighborhood had nefarious plans for them. If a neighbor had given any of the neighborhood boys a hard time for any reason, a snake might be placed in their mailbox. The mailboxes in most of the homes in those days were not out front like they are today; they went right into the house, so you had to reach inside your house in order to extract the mail the postman had left that day. Imagine the neighbor's surprise when, instead of pulling out a letter from Aunt Tilly or a bill from the water company, they put their hands on a slimy garter snake! How often this actually happened I don't recall, but I know it did.

Snakes, though, were not the only amphibians we utilized in our pranks. Frogs also came into play. One year, my brother sold a few of the frogs we had caught in northern Wisconsin and transported back to Chicago to a neighborhood pal, "Wayo." How did he get the nickname Wayo?" you might ask. Well, apparently, it was from his habit of running backward while yelling "Wayo, Wayo, Wayo." Why he did this, I have no idea. My brother remembers that Wayo wore a black leather jacket and greased down his hair with butter like the Fonz, the character played by Henry Winkler in the American sitcom *Happy Days*. Wayo snuck the frogs into the local Walgreens at 87th Street and South Cottage Grove, where he let them go. At the time, we thought this was humorous.

I remember visiting the Walgreens after their release and seeing several of them hopping around the aisles. In retrospect, I wish Joe had not sold the frogs to Wayo. It was certainly cruel for the poor frogs, and I imagine the Walgreens management did not appreciate the stunt. But, hey, we were kids growing up on the South Side of Chicago in the 1950s. By the way, the Walgreens is still there.

The most serious childhood mailbox prank, though, did not involve a snake or a frog but rather a firecracker. One of our childhood palls whom shall remain anonymous decided he would throw a lighted one into a neighbor's mailbox. He undoubtedly did this because the people who lived there had for some reason irked him. When the firecracker exploded, it did several hundred dollars' worth of damage to the house. How the neighbor discovered that our pal was the culprit I do not remember, but his father had to pay for the damage. It was the talk of the neighborhood for several weeks.

Though our mischievous behavior was relatively harmless, falling into the category of "boys will be boys" (one of the favorite sayings of parents in our neighborhood to excuse our bad behavior), it is important to observe that Chatham-Avalon was, to a large extent, a tranquil oasis surrounded by tougher neighborhoods. Chicago, like most big urban areas, has always been a city of ethnic enclaves. And, much like rival groups in *West Side Story*, you did not want to wander into certain Chicago neighborhoods in the 1950s if you belonged to a different clan. There were tough Irish gangs, Polish gangs, and Italian gangs, to name a few, in the Chicago of my youth. Chicago Vocational High School, located about five miles from where we lived, was notoriously rough. Perhaps one of CVS's toughest graduates was Dick Butkus, the legendary middle linebacker for the Chicago Bears from 1965 to 1973. Butkus grew up in the Roseland neighborhood south of Chatham-Avalon. My brother remembered playing against Butkus in a high school basketball game between Hirsch High School and CVS. Dick was not much of a basketball player, but the CVS coach put him in the game to "rough up" my brother who, at the time, was Hirsch's star player.

The Vanishing World Of My Chicago Childhood

**Joe Zucker Hirsch High School scoring against Chicago Vocational
High School 1958
Source: Zucker Family Photo
Credit Charles Jarmul**

Hirsch itself was a pretty tough high school. Although I only attended for one semester before we moved to the suburbs, my brother graduated from Hirsch in 1959—the same year I graduated from Dixon Elementary School. My brother's experience growing up on the South Side, in fact, was quite different than mine because he was four years older. So while I was just entering my teenage years before we moved to the suburbs, Joe had already graduated from high school.

By 1959, the student population was pretty much evenly divided between whites and African Americans. The school had its own security police officer because fights were not uncommon. Every so often, the word would spread that a gang war had been scheduled between an African American gang and an Italian gang at Grand Crossing Park, directly across the street from Hirsch. How many of these gang wars actually took place, I do not know. But there was talk in the halls at Hirsch of rival gang members making "zip guns" to shoot each other.

I got into (well, almost) only one altercation during my semester at Hirsch. Another student (who I admit was much smaller than me) was really bugging me in a class we took together. What he said that bothered me I do not remember, but I decided I would punch him after the class was over and confronted him out in the hallway. Fortunately, before any punches were thrown, some students intervened, warning me that I would be suspended for fighting. And that was that.

Years later, when I was a student in a creative writing class at the University of Wisconsin, we read a short story about an inner city high school. The instructor asked the class what we thought of the story. One of my classmates allowed that the story was ridiculous—that there could never be a high school that crazy. At the same time, my hand and the hand of an African American woman shot up, and we blurted out simultaneously, "Oh, yes there could!" We discovered later we had both attended Hirsch.

CHAPTER III
Indoor Games and Activities

Of course, the weather in Chicago during the winter months was frequently downright nasty—cold and snowy with howling winds blowing in off Lake Michigan. So from November through March, most of our games and activities took place indoors. As I believe was the case with our outdoor activities, the sheer number and variety of things that occupied the children in our neighborhood during the 1950s far exceeds the average among children today. Most importantly, except for a few activities such as reading, our indoor play involved actual interaction with my brother and my friends.

Sports Activities: Basketball, Hockey, and Fencing

As fall turned to winter, many of the sports activities that my brother and I enjoyed outside simply moved indoors—albeit in a somewhat truncated form. We were lucky because our home—like almost all those in our neighborhood—had a large unfinished basement. Our basement was perhaps forty feet long, thirty feet wide, and irregular in shape. Along the back wall in the northwest corner was the previously mentioned root cellar; in the southwest corner were the washer and dryer—primitive by today's standards. The furnace and water heater occupied a space along the north wall. But even with these impediments, we still had plenty of space to play. On the northeast side of the basement, we put up a backboard and basketball net. Since the ceiling was only around eight feet high, the net was perhaps around six feet above the floor. Still, this allowed for exciting basketball matchups between my brother and me—most of which he won, being four years older and quite athletic. We each even had our own imaginary high school basketball leagues with, if memory serves, eight teams. Each team had its own roster of players, and we kept count of wins and losses. And, of course, each of us had our favorite teams. What strikes me about this today is the imagination it took to create the two leagues. My brother, of course, would grow up to be a renowned artist with an international reputation, and as a child, he had a phenomenal imagination. But I was not left with the short end of the stick when it came to imagination. Much of our play had to do with make-believe. With the rise of electronic games in the last few decades, I wonder if children today use their imaginations as much as we did.

Hockey was another popular game we played in the basement. (No, we did not flood it.) We set up homemade goals on the east and west side of the room and fashioned our own hockey sticks out of old broomsticks with pieces of wood nailed to them. On our feet, we wore slipper socks, which were quite common in the fifties and gave us a little bit of the feel of being on ice skates. We did use an actual hockey puck purchased at a sporting goods store. We would face off at "center ice," and then the game was on. Baseball, too, was a sport we played in the basement, though our games were extremely limited in scope by the confines of our "field." Of course, some other activities that we played outside were easily transported indoors, such as hide-and-go-seek.

One sport that we played only indoors was fencing. At some point in our childhood, my brother and I saw an ad for fencing swords in a magazine. Although my mother never allowed us to own a BB gun because she thought them too dangerous, we were allowed to send away for the fencing swords. We were ecstatic when they arrived in the mail a few weeks later. Now, these swords were nothing like the modern fencing weapons you see advertised online today. The blades were perhaps four feet long and had little rubber balls attached to the tips. The balls were designed to prevent one fencer from doing real harm to their opponent. We had none of the other gear that serious fencers wear: a mask, a jacket, or a glove. The problem with the little balls was they kept falling off the ends of the blades. This did not stop my brother and me from engaging in hours of furious duels. We were lucky that neither of us suffered the loss of an eye. As I mentioned earlier, both my boys became highly skilled competitive fencers as young men who fenced for their college teams.

Board Games: Monopoly, Game of the States, Clue, and More

We also played a huge number of nonsporting games inside during the winter months (and also during the summer months when we were tired of playing outdoors). Board games were among the most popular. Generally, it took more than two kids, though, so we had to round up some of our neighborhood pals. This was generally not done by phone. Rather, we simply walked to a neighbor's house, knocked on the side door, and asked if the pal could come out and play. This, of course, was the preferred way of getting a group of friends together to play, whether it was for an inside or an outside game. The concept of parents arranging a "playdate" was unknown. So I would recruit a few of my pals to play a board game with me and perhaps my brother.

What board games did we play? Some of them are still quite popular today; others have fallen by the wayside. Probably the one we played most was Monopoly, which first hit the market in 1933. Then, as is the case now, a Monopoly game could go on for hours until one player had bankrupted the others. My friend Calvin almost always won. Clue was another board game we often played. This one involves solving a murder in a large mansion. It has different characters, weapons, and locations. The players have to figure out which character committed the murder based on clues given by the others. It was first published in 1943, then updated with more modern artwork for reissues from 1948 to the present day. So if you thought you had the answer to who did the dastardly deed, you might announce, "It was Colonel Mustard in the library with the knife." If you were right, you won; if you were wrong, you were disqualified. Sorry, Parcheesi, and Game of the States were also popular.

I particularly liked Game of the States (1940), which a player won by transporting products by truck from one state to another, buying and selling them in hopes of making a profit. So, for example, you might pick up potatoes in Idaho and transport them to Florida, where you would sell your potatoes and purchase some grapefruit. The fifty cards (forty-eight in early editions) used in the game contain fun facts about each state. For example, by drawing the Michigan card in the 1940 edition, you would learn that Michigan (the Wolverine State) is home to 11,000 lakes and 36,000 miles of streams—more freshwater shoreline than any other state (except, of course, Alaska, which was not yet a state). You would also learn that the capital of Michigan is Lansing, and the state entered the Union in 1837. I am shocked today by people (some of them college grads) who are ignorant of the geography of the United States. Perhaps they ought to use Game of the States in the schools.

One of our favorite indoor games did involve a primitive form of electronics. It was a football game with little players who could move up and down the field, propelled along by the vibrations generated by a small electronic motor. The quarterback actually had a little spring-loaded throwing arm, and the game came with tiny felt footballs so the team on offense had the option of running the ball or passing. When I went online to research this game, I discovered it is still being sold today by Tudor Games. What a surprise!

Electronic football was invented in the 1940s by Norman Sas, the son of the company's founder. The model my brother and I played still had metal players and a relatively small field. Over the decades, the players, which are now made out of plastic, have become more sophisticated looking, and the field is larger. And you can customize your field so, for example, it could become the home of the Chicago Bears, Soldier's Field. Our model sold for around $16. Today, you can purchase the forty-eight-by-twenty-four-inch Ultimate Electric Football game with a brushed aluminum frame for as low as $249. Of course, the players and the field are much spiffier than what we had in the 1950s, but the game is basically the same. The Tudor website proudly announces that two books have been authored about the game.

Ice hockey was another tabletop sports game that Joe and I played endlessly. It was similar to electronic football, only you moved the players back and forward with levers as you attempted to score a goal with a little plastic puck. That game is still very much around as well; it's sold today by ManCave Games for around $139. Interestingly, in modern times, I have never seen children playing either the electronic football or the ice hockey game, but both companies are apparently doing a land-office business selling them, so they must be popular somewhere.

Reading, Music, Art, and Science

The typical white middle-class family of the 1950s has been widely viewed by critics as mindless and the overall culture of the 1950s as superficial—one that valued conformity above all else. All you have to do is watch reruns of the incredibly awful musical variety program *The Lawrence Welk Show*, first aired on TV in 1951, or *Your Hit Parade*, which debuted on TV in 1953, to see there is some truth to the critic's claims. But there was much more going on in many middle-class white families—including ours—than programs like those two would suggest. As Susan Jacoby argues in her marvelous book *The Age of American Unreason* (Pantheon Books, 2008), the 1950s was also a decade in which many parents valued learning and culture in a way that has declined in recent times. *Encyclopedia Britannica* sets sold briskly because parents wanted to have the wealth of information in them available to their children in an era long before the internet. This happened, above all, because many men and women who became parents in the 1950s had been denied the opportunity for cultural advancement themselves by the Great Depression and World War II. My mother, Leah, was a good example of that. She believed, above all, that children should have a general knowledge of everything, and travel in itself was highly educational. The valedictorian of her high school class in Antigo, Wisconsin, in 1925, she could not afford to go to college. As I mentioned earlier, she moved to Chicago instead, where she became a registered nurse, doing her training at Ravenswood Hospital on the North Side.

My mother was an avid reader. I wish I could tell you what sort of books she enjoyed, but, unfortunately, I don't remember. I think she favored murder mysteries. My brother and I both followed in her footsteps. What did I read? Of course, a lot of comic books. We had subscriptions to *Donald Duck, Uncle Scrooge, Mickey Mouse, Bugs Bunny*, and others. It might be hard for children today to understand how excited I was when a new edition of *Donald Duck* showed up in our mailbox. Later on, when TV came into vogue, we also watched animated versions of our favorites.

As I grew older, my reading interests expanded. I have already mentioned that *God is My Co-Pilot* was one of my favorites. Another was Sir Edmund Hillary's account of climbing the world's highest mountain—*High Adventure: The True Story of the First Ascent of Everest*, published in 1955. And then there was science fiction. My visits to the local public library often ended with me checking out several science fiction novels and short stories. My favorite authors (what a surprise) were Isaac Asimov and Robert Heinlein. We also received books as presents from my parents. One of my favorites was a book containing a potpourri of jokes, information about athletes, and games. I still tell some of the jokes today, much to the horror of family members. Another favorite was a book describing the freshwater fish of North America, complete with beautiful plates. It was actually given to my brother, who gifted it to me. I still own it today.

My brother and I were exposed to art, music, literature, and science. On several occasions, Joe and I took leaves of absence for a week before spring break from Dixon Elementary School (with the principal's blessing) to embark on extended road trips around the United States with our parents. Hanging on the wall in my study is a wonderful painting my brother did when he was in the seventh grade of the Zucker family driving through the Louisiana bayous in our 1953 Oldsmobile 98. We were on our way to Florida. On another vacation, we drove from Chicago to Los Angeles. And, of course, many other families were out exploring the USA on the new expanded highway system (like Route 66). My wife and her family drove from Chicago to Mexico City one summer. These were family vacations, above all, but they *were* educational. We learned a lot about the geography of the United States. As I mentioned earlier, I am often dumbstruck at what intelligent, college-educated younger people today do not know about our states, lakes, rivers, mountains, and cities.

My brother and I also listened to a wide range of music. Dixieland jazz was popular in the 1950s. I owned several albums by the Dukes of Dixieland. We also listened to a good deal of classical music performed by people like Arturo Rubenstein. And folk music started to become popular as I reached the eighth grade. The Kingston Trio's first album was a huge hit. One of the songs from it, "Tom Dooley," was released as a single, selling over a million records. This began my lifelong love of folk music.

We prided ourselves on what we knew. I hasten to add that the inspiration for learning in our family came from my mother. I have to admit I do not have a single memory of my father reading a book. His two passions remained going to Wrigley Field to watch a Chicago Cubs game and to Arlington Park to bet on the horses.

Chicago itself, of course, has a wealth of wonderful cultural and scientific institutions. The Museum of Science and Industry, Shedd Aquarium, the Adler Planetarium, the Field Museum, and the Art Institute of Chicago are all world-class institutions. My favorite (and I think that of most children) was the Museum of Science and Industry. In 1954, the museum received a U-505, a German submarine that had been captured in 1944. I remember the excitement in Chicago when the sub was transported down Michigan Avenue and installed in the museum. I must have walked through the U-505 a dozen times as a child and, later on, would take my own children to see it. My other favorite Museum of Science and Industry exhibit was the coal mine. After walking up about three flights of stairs, we would descend into the depths of the mine. It always was interesting and scary.

At the Shedd Aquarium, I marveled at the beautiful and exotic sea creatures on display. As an adult, I would become a scuba diver and have the opportunity to see them in their own environment. In large measure because of our visits to the Adler Planetarium, I developed a strong interest in astronomy. Peering into the recesses of the universe left me in a state of wonder. In eighth grade, the graduating elementary school students listed their chosen professions. I wanted to be an astronomer. My classmate, Steve T., and I spent weeks constructing a star chart that won honorable mention in our school's science fair. Unfortunately, I was not destined to become an astronomer for two good reasons: I was extremely nearsighted and had only mediocre math skills.

The Field Museum perhaps was geared more toward adults, but I still remember staring at the Egyptian mummy exhibit. Finally, there was the Art Institute of Chicago. The Art Institute was undoubtedly more important in my brother's upbringing than mine. My mother recognized early on that Joe exhibited extraordinary art talent. Many of my early memories are sitting at the kitchen table with him, drawing and painting. Some parents might have discouraged their child's art talent, but my mother did not. He was still a preteen when my mother enrolled him in classes at the Art Institute. He would go on to earn his master's degree and later an honorary PhD from the Art Institute. Today several of his paintings are in the Art Institute's collections.

The Zucker Family Gets a TV (The Beginning of the End?)

When I began thinking about the role TV played in my childhood, I had a revelation: watching TV was much more important for the Zucker family than I had remembered. My best guess is that we purchased our first TV in the early 1950s. It was, of course, a black-and-white console TV with a screen measuring probably somewhere around fifteen inches. It was placed in the living room. The TV soon became a center of Zucker family activity. We received four stations (channels 2, 5, 7, and 9), and somewhere along the way, an educational channel (11) was added. Later on, a host of UHF channels were added. In the early days of TV, there were often significant amounts of time between programs. So we would frequently sit in front of the set watching the test pattern until one started.

My children believe the infotainment revolution began with their generation, but I believe it actually began during my generation with the introduction of TV. TV was first available to Americans prior to WWII, but it was only after the war ended that Americans began to purchase TVs in significant numbers. According to Wikipedia, in 1950, almost four million American households (9 percent) had TVs. Over the next ten years, the numbers exploded: By 1955, there were nearly thirty-one million (about 65 percent), and by 1960, nearly forty-six million (about 87 percent). Of course, the number of TV stations, channels, and programs grew rapidly to meet the surging demand. Three major networks—NBC, ABC, and CBS—provided the majority of TV programming. As Americans began watching more and more TV, other popular forms of entertainment declined. Book sales and movie attendance, for example, dropped off. It also began to affect Americans' behavior. By the mid-1970s, the term "couch potato," meaning a lazy person who watches TV all day, entered the American language. (I myself have been accused of being a card-carrying member of the couch potato nation. I hasten to add that the accusation is without any merit whatsoever.)

I could launch into a long history of TV programs popular in the 1950s and early 1960s, but I would rather focus on the ones I remember watching with my family. Of course, there were several different genres. For my brother and me, Westerns were a big deal. Among our favorites were *Hopalong Cassidy*, *The Lone Ranger*, and *The Roy Rogers Show*. Of course, I (like most boys in the 1950s) had a Western outfit and a six-shooter cap gun. One of our favorite children's programs was *The Howdy Doody Show*, starring Buffalo Bob Smith and Clarabell the Clown. Clarabell wore a baggy striped costume and communicated through mime and by honking a horn for yes or no. Three actors played Clarabelle on a regular basis. The first was Bob Keeshan, who later became the star of *Captain Kangaroo*—another very popular kids' program.

Science fiction was another favorite genre for my brother and me. After dinner, we would watch *Captain Video and the Video Rangers*, a very early attempt at putting science fiction on TV. To say it was primitive would be an understatement. Another favorite was *Flash Gordon*. The plot was simple. An evil dictator on a planet that had somehow positioned itself near Earth was causing the catastrophic disruption of the atmosphere. Flash and his sidekicks must travel to the planet via their spaceship to save Earth. Who can forget that list of memorable characters? In addition to Flash himself, there was Dale Arden, his love interest; Dr. Hans Zarkov, the scientist; the evil Ming the Merciless; Princess Aura, his daughter; and many others. Based on a comic strip by the same name, thirty-nine episodes were produced, and the program aired on TV in 1954. At the time I watched it, the sets seemed realistic to me. Now, of course, it is hilarious to watch the reruns.

But the early TV programs that were destined to transform American culture were the evening variety shows. Perhaps the most famous of these was the *Texaco Star Theater* (1948–1953) starring comedian Milton Berle, which aired on Tuesday nights. As the host of the program, Berle was the first major television star and was known to millions of viewers as "Uncle Miltie" and "Mr. Television." Like so many early TV stars,

Berle started his career as a vaudeville performer and then transitioned to television.

Another Zucker family favorite was the iconic *Ed Sullivan Show*, which ran from its inception in 1948 on CBS from eight to nine p.m. Eastern time until its cancellation in 1971. Sullivan did not come from a performance background. He was a journalist and proved to be rather stiff in front of the cameras. But this only seemed to add to his charm. His TV audiences loved him. Virtually every type of entertainment appeared on the show: classical musicians, opera singers, popular recording artists, songwriters, comedians, ballet dancers, and dramatic actors. The show enjoyed phenomenal success as the American family (including the Zuckers) gathered around the TV set on Sunday evening to watch the acts. The blockbuster performers who appeared on the *Ed Sullivan Show* included Elvis Presley, Buddy Holly, the Jackson 5, and, of course, the Beatles. Since it was our family tradition to eat our Sunday dinner in the afternoon around one p.m., my mother would prepare a light supper of cold cuts (salami, bologna, etc.), cheese, and other assorted snacks for us to enjoy as we watched the *Ed Sullivan Show* in the living room on Sunday evening.

Many of the other wonderful TV programs the Zucker family watched together started out life as radio programs but then segued in the 1950s into the new medium. One of the most successful of these was *The Jack Benny Program*. It was telecast on CBS from October 28, 1950, to September 15, 1964. It became a weekly show in the 1960–1961 season and was on NBC from September 25, 1964, to September 10, 1965. We loved this program with its incredible cast of characters, including his wife, played by Mary Livingston; his butler Rochester, played by the African American actor Eddie Anderson; his announcer, Don Wilson; and a host of other performers. Although the program was always partially a variety show, over the years, it evolved into a situation comedy.

Comedian Bob Hope's TV specials were also mainstays of the Zuckers' TV viewing. And who can forget *The Dinah Shore Show*, broadcast by NBC from November 1951 to July 1957 and sponsored by General Motors's Chevrolet division? *The Cavalcade of Stars* starring Jackie Gleason was another Zucker family favorite. Gleason, who may just have been the most gifted comedian of the twentieth century, played a number of different recurring characters during the program, including the friendly Joe the bartender; the playboy millionaire Reginald Van Gleason III; a sad-sack character, "the Poor Soul"; and, most famously, the blowhard Brooklyn bus driver Ralph Kramden. In fact, the Kramden character was so hilarious that Gleason turned the skit into a half-hour sitcom, *The Honeymooners*. Audrey Meadows played Gleason's wife, Alice, and Art Carney played the upstairs neighbor Ed Norton, who worked for the city's sewer system. The series ran from 1955 to 1956 with a total of thirty-nine programs.

Everyone's favorite sitcom, though, was *I Love Lucy*, starring Lucille Ball as Lucy; Desi Arnaz, her husband in real life; and Vivian Vance and William Frawley as Ethel and Fred Mertz, respectively—Lucy and Desi's landlords. It originally aired on CBS from October 1951 to May 1957—a total of 180 half-hour episodes. *I Love Lucy* was the most-watched show on TV for four of its six seasons.

As my years residing at 8610 Rhodes Avenue were drawing to a close, *Shock Theater* emerged as one of my favorite TV program. The program aired Saturday nights at ten p.m. on Chicago's WBKB from 1957 to 1959. The host was Marvin, a demented beatnik, played by Terry Bennett. *Shock Theater* presented a variety of awful horror films. Bennett frequently poked fun at the movies, drawing howls of laughter from my pals and me as we watched while munching pizza in front of a second Zucker TV that sat in our breakfast room.

My wife Shaya's experience watching television as a child growing up in the suburb of Lincolnwood north of Chicago mirrored my own. Perhaps she and her brother were even more mesmerized by the TV than the Zucker lads. I have often heard the story about how her father became so exasperated with their constant TV viewing that he cut the electrical cord to the set. Below is a wonderful photo of Shaya and brother, Craig, dressed up in their cowboy outfits in front of the family's first television.

**Shaya and her brother, Craig, standing in front of the Gornstein family TV in their cowboy outfits.
(Source: Zucker Family Photo)**

Sporting Events on TV

Watching sporting events on TV became another major focus of Zucker family life—at least for the three Zucker men. This was especially true when it came to viewing the Chicago Cubs games on WGN's Channel 9. The first game televised was in 1948 between the Cubs and their crosstown rivals, the White Sox. The legendary Jack Brickhouse announced the games from the late 1940s until 1981. Since Wrigley Field would not install lights for evening games until 1988, all the Cubs' home games were played during the day. This meant that during the school year, brother Joe and I could only watch the later innings of their games. My memory, though, is that we did not rush home from Dixon Elementary to turn on the TV to see the last three innings or so. We both preferred playing outside if the weather was nice.

One exception was the day (May 12, 1955) that Sam Jones pitched a no-hitter at Wrigley for the Cubs against the Pittsburgh Pirates, winning 4–0. Jones was the first African American pitcher in the major leagues to pitch a no-hitter. Somehow, the word spread at Dixon Elementary that he had a no-hitter going against the Pirates through seven innings. We dashed home and turned on the TV to watch the exciting conclusion to the game. Of course, watching a Cub game from the first pitch through the final out was not a problem during summer vacations. In fact, we watched dozens of complete Cub games through the years long after the Zuckers had moved from 8610 Rhodes Avenue to our new home in the suburbs. It was a family ritual. Of course, baseball games were much shorter in duration back then—perhaps two and half hours—as opposed to games today that frequently last an hour longer than that. In fact, as I am writing this, Major League Baseball has instituted a bunch of changes to speed up the game.

We also watched professional football games. Although the first pro football game was telecast in 1939, the first NFL championship game to be televised was in 1948 between the Philadelphia Eagles and the Chicago Cardinals. Pro football games on TV were few and far between compared to today. I remember how excited the three men in the Zucker household became when Thanksgiving drew near because the Bears would be playing one of their archenemies, like the Detroit Lions or the Green Bay Packers. The games at that time of year were often played in horrendous weather, adding to their drama.

We watched professional basketball as well, though that sport was yet in its infancy compared to today. I remember watching stars like Big George Mikan, center for the Minneapolis Lakers, and Bob Cousy, guard for the incomparable Boston Celtics. Finally, there was boxing—an enormously popular TV sport in the 1950s. The Zucker men loved to watch the *Gillette Friday Night Fights*. I remember seeing legendary boxers, including Sugar Ray Robinson, Rocky Marciano, Jersey Joe Walcott, Archie Moore, Ezzard Charles, and Floyd Patterson, among others. I still enjoy watching an occasional pugilistic contest on TV today.

Although I believe the number of hours the Zucker family watched TV in the 1950s was, on average, far below the number of hours that families spend in front of the TV today, there's no doubt it changed how we spent our leisure time enormously. Watching TV was enjoyable: the kids' shows, the variety and comedy programs, the sporting events, and more added to the quality of the Zucker family members' lives. But it also accelerated the disturbing trend toward the isolation of Americans from one another. As we began to spend more time peering at the TV, we spent less time with friends and neighbors. It was then—and is today—a double-edged sword.

My Mother's Cooking

Family meals, of course, were important for the Zuckers, just as they are for millions of American families today. And no childhood memoir could be complete without talking about my mother's cooking. For breakfast, what I remember eating was mainly processed cereals such as Rice Krispies, cornflakes, or Grape-Nuts; orange juice; milk; and bacon before brother Joe and I rushed off to Dixon Elementary. I still remember pouring a bowl of cereal from the Wheaties box that had the image of the Olympic hero Reverend Bob Richards on the front with the motto "Breakfast of Champions." I returned home for lunch and generally would have had a peanut butter and jelly or perhaps a bologna sandwich. On most evenings, we had dinner in our kitchen dining area. On Sundays, we generally had a bigger spread in the dining room in the early afternoon, followed by a lighter meal in the evening.

My mother was a fine cook. As a child growing up in northern Wisconsin, she learned to cook basic meals—nothing fancy. So we often had dishes like pork chops, hamburgers, meatloaf, chicken, fried liver, and so on as the main dish, along with a salad, a cooked vegetable, and more. On special occasions, she went all out. In a conversation I had with brother Joe, who remembered more about her cooking than I do, he raved about his favorites: roast turkey (undoubtedly on Thanksgiving Day), prime rib of beef, chili, spaghetti and meatballs, and chicken and dumplings. There was one exception to her fine cooking. I don't know why, but my mother's mashed potatoes were gosh-darned awful. I remember her pouring milk in with the potatoes and mixing the concoction with a hand blender. They turned out lumpy and unappetizing. It would be many years before I learned that mashed potatoes could actually be quite tasty.

Today, I have very few of my mother's possessions. But one thing I do have is a little tin box containing some of her recipes. A few of them have a printed inscription—"From the Kitchen Of" or "Here's What's Cooking," with a place for the chef to write their name in. One of them contains the recipe for "Leah's molasses cookies (gingerbread)" and another "Leah, Nola" for a "salad mold." So my mother and her sister-in-law, Aunt Nola, were obviously sharing favorite recipes.

My mother made fabulous cookies. This probably explains why I went from being a scrawny infant to a chubby twelve-year-old. My favorite cookies were her almond crescents, which my brother and I called worms. We also fondly recall her rice pudding. But my absolute favorite dessert was the mincemeat pie with warm brandy topping she made only when company came for dinner.

While we lived on the South Side, we did not own a barbecue grill. In fact, I do not remember any of our neighbors grilling outdoors. Barbecuing outdoors would become a Zucker ritual after we moved to the suburbs. Of course, it is usually the man's job to toss the steaks on the grill, and Irv did, indeed, learn to do that after we had moved to 6800 Kedvale Avenue in Lincolnwood. However, I do not remember my father actually preparing a dinner for my brother and me while we resided at 8610 Rhodes Avenue. On those rare evenings when Leah went out somewhere for the evening, he would open a can of corned beef hash, which he emptied into a frying pan. (Come to think of it, the fried hash was pretty tasty.)

Once in a while, we were invited to dinner at a neighbor's house. I remember dining at Calvin and Jeff's house. Their mother made the most wonderful Swiss steak. The American family's eating habits seem to have changed dramatically since I was a kid. For one thing, men in middle-class families prepare more of the evening meals now because of the advent of both mom and dad working. Then, too, families eat out at fast food joints much more than when I was growing up. I don't remember the Zuckers ever going out for dinner at a place like McDonalds or Chick-fil-A. Also, now it's common in the two-working-parent family to order preprepared meals that arrive at your front door.

CHAPTER IV

Two Institutions That Shaped My Youth: Arthur Dixon Elementary School and Sinai Congregation

Two institutions had a major impact on my childhood. One was Arthur Dixon Elementary School, where I began my education in kindergarten, graduating from the eighth grade in January 1959. The second was Sinai Temple, where I received my upbringing as a member of the Jewish faith.

Dixon Elementary School

The Arthur Dixon Elementary School is an imposing structure located at 8306 Lawrence Avenue. Named for a Chicago businessman and alderman, the school opened its doors in 1929. Like many of the city's schools from this era, it looks like a fortress. It's constructed of brick and is three floors high. Dixon is less than four blocks from where the Zucker family resided at 8610 Rhodes Avenue, and it is a straight shot down Rhodes to get to the school. So it was easy for my brother and me to walk to and from school. A lot of kids still walk to school, even today. What has changed, though, is that we did this not just once a day, but *twice* per day. Why, you might ask, did we walk back and forth to school twice? The answer is simple: we came home for lunch. In fact, if memory serves, Dixon did not have a cafeteria. I am not sure what the heck kids did if, for some reason or another, they could not go home for lunch. The fact is that I do not remember anyone who stayed at school during the lunch hour, though there must have been some. Maybe they brought their lunch with them in a little lunch pail.

In any case, around noon, a bunch of kids would walk back home from Dixon to eat lunch at home. My sandwich, prepared by my mother, would be waiting for me. If I were lucky, a brand-new Donald Duck, Uncle Scrooge, or Bugs Bunny comic book would have arrived in the mail that morning, which I would read while munching on my sandwich. Soon, it would be time to head back to school. Around three-thirty p.m. or so, school would be out, and we would all walk home again.

Our neighborhood had a substantial Catholic population, and the children of these families generally did not attend a public school but rather went to a parochial school. But the drill was pretty much the same for them. One difference was the Catholic kids dressed in uniforms whereas we did not.

My educational experience at Dixon did not start out well. To tell the truth, I was something of a mama's boy who was pretty much attached to my mother's apron strings. As a small child, I was sickly and something of a runt. In fact, our next-door neighbor to the north of us used to ask my mother, "How on Earth are you ever going to raise that child?" So when it came time for me to start school, I was terrified at the prospect of leaving the nurturing environment of my home.

Finding myself in kindergarten was traumatic. What made matters worse was my kindergarten teacher, Miss H. I hated her. Okay, I know, kindergarten teachers are supposed to be universally sweet and loving. She was not. In fact, I remember telling my mother that Miss H. "only smiles with her mouth," by which I meant she was not really smiling—it was a facade. I did not want to be in school. I wanted to be back home.

So not too long after school started in the fall, I made a run for it. This happened a long, long time ago—I don't remember a lot of the details. What I do remember is that I was intercepted somewhere on my way home. I also know that I was forced to go back to kindergarten the next day. To make matters worse, I was not a good kindergarten student. One of the requirements for passing kindergarten was learning how to skip. I had an enormous amount of trouble learning to do this. Finally, I mastered the skill. I still like to tell people that I came very close to failing kindergarten. Perhaps I have inherited my father's self-deprecating sense of humor.

Fortunately, kindergarten turned out to be an anomaly in my years at Dixon. My first and second grade teachers were wonderful, and I began to blossom as a student. I learned how to read easily and became a good student whose report cards were filled with Es and Gs. And after my bad start in kindergarten, my classroom behavior was good. This was not true of my brother who was four years ahead of me. It seemed that he was always getting in trouble for some form of mischievous behavior. My mother had to make frequent trips to school to talk to the principal or one of his teachers. His shenanigans made life a little bit tougher for me. More than one teacher asked me on the first day of class, "You are Joe Zucker's brother?" with a look of consternation on their faces.

More than six decades have passed since I last attended Dixon, so my recollection of who my teachers were in each grade and what I learned is pretty foggy. But I do have some memories. First, all my teachers were women except for Mr. M., who taught PE. And although I don't know for sure, I believe many of them were single women. Remember, this was a time well before the women's liberation movement changed things for middle-class white women. In terms of professional careers, educated women were pretty much limited to fields such as teaching, nursing, social work, and library science. This, in fact, would not change much until after I had graduated from college (1966). How old were these women teachers? Of course, as a child, they all seemed old to me. My guess is that most of them were at least in their thirties. They were there for the long haul—not just teaching for a year or two until they got married.

A second factor is that I attended grammar school during the height of the Cold War, a period of enormous tension between the Western democracies and the Soviet Union. This was the era of the Berlin Wall, the H-bomb, the Korean War, and the "kitchen debate" between Soviet Premier Nikita Khrushchev and Vice President Richard Nixon. The fear that communism would spread throughout the world caused a good deal of paranoia in the United States. Communist cells were thought to be at work infiltrating American institutions, including the government. One of the most popular TV programs during this era was *I Led Three Lives*, which ran from 1953 to 1956. The program was based loosely on the life of Herbert Philbrick, a Boston advertising agent who was a double agent for the FBI.

As a result, the US began to defend itself not only militarily but also both at home and abroad through expositions about how wonderful life was in America. I do not remember any really heavy-handed propaganda emanating from my teachers at Dixon or from our reading assignments, though what we learned about our nation was cast in a positive light. We were taught that America was a nation of immigrants who had come together to form one nation out of many—e pluribus unum. Examples were given of immigrants who had made remarkable contributions to American society. Of course, sometimes the lessons tended to be far fetched. I remember reading in one of our books, for example, that Americans were lucky because we all got to eat white bread while people in the rest of the world had to eat coarse "dark bread." At the time, I was struck by how fortunate we were. Now, of course, I know better. The main advantage of white bread over dark bread is that it can be stored for longer periods of time without becoming rancid. It is not nearly as healthy as that "awful" dark bread that people in poor countries were forced to consume.

Perhaps the Cold War culture I grew up in also had something to do with how much we studied US history and government at Dixon. Later on, I would realize that, of course, the history we learned in grade school had been sanitized. Subjects like slavery, the genocide committed against Native Americans, and the struggles of working-class people were glossed over or worse. But, nonetheless, by the time I graduated from Dixon, I knew a lot about American history. In fact, I would argue I probably knew more than most students graduating from American high schools today and probably more than many graduating from college.

We also knew a great deal about the geography of the United States. We studied maps and state capitals. We also studied English grammar and learned how to diagram sentences. By the time we reached seventh grade, we began to have specialized classes. We had art, for example. And, of course, we had PE. I know we also studied math because I remember struggling with learning how to do division somewhere around the fifth grade.

Of course, we had recess. I remember being turned loose in the mornings for half an hour to run amok with the other kids in the gravel playground. In addition to recess, we also had movies once a week in Dixon's impressive auditorium. What I remember about these movies is that they were weird by present-day standards. Several of them were quite scary. I remember one, for example, where trolls came out of a river and ran after children. I think that these movies were a product of a culture in which traditional fairy tales, which are often quite frightening, were more popular than they are today. The online Britannica, for example, defines a troll in early Scandinavian folklore as a giant, monstrous being, sometimes possessing magic powers. Britannica adds that trolls in modern tales for children often live under bridges, menacing travelers, and exacting tasks or tolls. For the life of me, I am unable to figure out what educational purpose these movies served. I suspect they gave the teachers a needed break from dealing with their charges.

What was it like inside the classroom at Dixon? I remember the classrooms were traditional. We each had our own desk, and the desks were arranged in tidy rows. The students often sat in alphabetical order, which meant, more often than not, I was at the back of the room. The teacher sat up front behind her desk, and behind her was a blackboard. I am sure there was also an American flag somewhere in the room. The classes each had around twenty to thirty pupils. I remember discipline being strict, but at least we were spared the corporal punishment that was often inflicted by the nuns on our friends who attended Catholic schools when they misbehaved. Of course, if you misbehaved at Dixon, you were sent to the principal's office. I don't remember ever being sent there. I wish I could remember the principal's name, but it has escaped me. I would like to walk the halls at Dixon one more time, but I don't know if that will happen.

Interestingly, Neal Samors's wonderful collection of stories entitled *Memories of Growing Up in Chicago: Recalling Life during the 20th Century* (Chicago's Neighborhood Press, 2024) contains a lovely essay by Norman Mark about growing up in the Chatham neighborhood. In fact, our family knew the Mark family. Norman was a contemporary of my brother, graduating from both Dixon and Hirsch High School. I particularly loved his description of his years at Dixon and Hirsch, which closely mirrored my own experiences at the two schools. Norman went on from Hirsch to graduate from Northwestern University's Medill School of Journalism. He was an award-winning film critic and entertainment reporter. His essay is well worth reading. He passed away in 2012.

How did my public school education from kindergarten through eighth grade differ from today? You will not be surprised by my impression that, in many ways, things have gone downhill. What I find most astounding is the lack of knowledge that even high school students and, yes, college students have about the country they live in. This fact was perhaps best popularized by late-night comedian Jay Leno's segment "Jaywalking," in which he went out onto the street to ask young people questions about the United States. Their ignorance was appalling. For example, some had no idea how many US senators there are, or what is contained in the Bill of Rights. Others could not name a foreign country that bordered the United States.

I have had personal experiences with this ignorance. After retiring in 2007, I volunteered for several years at the Bob Bullock Texas State Historical Museum in Austin. On many days, the museum was packed with students, generally ranging from the fourth grade through high school. The most impressive exhibit in the Bullock is the shipwreck of the *La Belle*, one of the many boats in the explorer La Salle's ill-fated 1684 expedition to the New World. La Salle was a consummate trader who hoped to make a fortune exchanging beads, jewelry, hatchets, and so forth for the valuable furs that Native Americans had in abundance. The *La Belle* contained millions of trade good items, and many of them, painstakingly recovered, are displayed in cases. I liked to stand in front of these display cases and ask the students with whom La Salle planned to trade? When they could not answer the question, I gave them a hint: "Who," I would ask, "was in the New World before the Europeans arrived?" Most of them had no idea. Maybe there was some excuse for the fourth graders but not for the older students.

The lack of knowledge of American geography is also staggering. Several years ago, I made a phone call to our internet provider to inform the company that since we would be leaving for our summer home in Montana, I needed to suspend our service in Austin. The woman I was talking to seemed puzzled by my request, which I repeated several times. Actually, she seemed downright annoyed. Finally, she blurted out to me, "What's Montana?"

I thought for a second and then asked her calmly where she was located. She informed me she was in upstate New York. I asked her if she had a computer at home. She replied that she did. So I suggested that when she went home that night, she should pull up a map of the United States, and she would see that Montana is the fourth-largest state in the nation. I did not have the nerve to ask her if she was a college grad. I was afraid the answer might be yes.

Several years ago, when we still lived in Austin, a TV repairman came out to our house. We somehow got to talking about American ignorance. He said that for several years, he had worked as a troubleshooter for Apple computers at a call-in center. On many occasions, the Apple client would ask him where he was located. "In New Mexico," he would reply. There would be silence for a moment. Then the perplexed person would say, "But you speak such good English. In what part of Mexico is New Mexico located?"

In my view, though, by far the most dangerous aspect of American ignorance is the lack of knowledge not just of American history but, even more important, of how our government works. Again, at Dixon, American history and civics were subjects I believe we were taught in every grade. We knew we lived in a democracy and why that was important. Again, I am aware the United States had many serious faults in the 1950s (and it still does today). Yet that fact does not negate the importance our system of government has had for our citizens historically. Surveys today routinely show that a large percentage of Americans don't give a hoot if they live in a democratic system of government. I believe this is because American history and civics were largely neglected when they were in school. When I asked my fellow volunteers at the Bullock, many of whom were former grade school teachers, why the kids who came through the museum seemed to know so little about these subjects, they blamed it on the mania for standardized testing, which has been a huge part of Texas K–12 education for decades. They told me teachers have to "teach to the test." If their students do not do well on them, they could be fired. And the standardized tests do not cover subjects like history, civics, and geography.

Then, too, part of the problem may be generational. I grew up in a scary world. The Nazis had just been defeated after a horrible war that saw six million Jews murdered in the Holocaust and countless more non-Jewish civilians killed. The Soviet Union, which was hell-bent on destroying democracies like the United States, was a very real and present danger. My point is simply that a large proportion of the American public today does not seem to value living in a democratic society, and much of the blame may lie with our schools.

Sinai Temple

At some point, my father and mother decided a religious upbringing would be good for my brother and me, so they joined Sinai Temple. When my parents married, my mother converted from Protestantism to Judaism. Many of my Wisconsin relatives were Protestants but others were Catholics. My parents were married at Temple Sholom on July 3, 1935, so my dad would have been thirty-one and my mother twenty-seven. For some reason, it is hard for me to imagine they were once that young. I remember them telling my brother and me they honeymooned at the famous Edgewood Beach Hotel in Chicago. I wish I knew more about their wedding. Who was my father's best man? Who attended the wedding?

Since my father's relatives came from Western Europe (Germany, Austria, etc.), they were assimilationist Jews who sought to blend in with the wider culture in which they lived. They tended to be educated and cultured and considered themselves fully members of the nations in which they lived. This was especially true when, in many European countries, most discriminatory restrictions against Jews were removed as a result of Enlightenment era reforms. Western European Jews had pretty much abandoned the old ways. Intermarriage was not uncommon. Many assimilated Jews celebrated Christmas. They stood in marked contrast to the far more numerous Jews in Eastern Europe (Poland, the Ukraine, etc.), who lived in small Jewish communities or *shtetls* and stuck to the old ways. Anyone who has seen the movie *Fiddler on the Roof* has a good idea of what life was like in these communities. In fact, in America, there was a good deal of tension between the two groups. The educated Western European Jews tended to look down their noses at their poor country cousins from the shtetls while the Eastern European Jews did not consider their assimilated brethren to be bona fide members of the religion.

Founded in 1861, Sinai Temple was perhaps the penultimate reform congregation in Chicago. According to documents from the American Jewish Archives, available online, the congregation's mission was "to serve the more religiously liberal German Jews on the south side of Chicago." Sinai's first rabbi, Bernhard Felsenthal, and other leading members of the congregation believed they should not stand on tradition and felt reforms and institutions should be changed to meet modern conditions. In practice, this meant Sinai's services were unlike anything you would find in an Orthodox Jewish shul.

If you have ever been to an Orthodox service or perhaps seen one in a movie, you know that men and women are strictly segregated. At Temple Sinai, men and women sat together. Moreover, the services were largely in English with a lot of transliteration from Hebrew. And there was an organ—something you would never find in a Conservative or Orthodox congregation. To top it all off, Sinai threw out the window the traditional bar mitzvah, by which Jewish boys transition to manhood at the age of thirteen or fourteen. As you may know, a bar mitzvah involves reading a portion of the Torah (the first five books of the bible) in Hebrew. This is quite an ordeal in the United States, where most Jewish boys and girls do not grow up reading and writing in Hebrew as they do in Israel. What is more, back in the 1950s, bar mitzvahs, as was the tradition, were reserved for boys only. Instead of having a bar mitzvah, we had a confirmation service equally available to both sexes.

In 1923, Emil G. Hirsch, one of Sinai's great rabbis, passed away. Hirsch was a social reformer who worked closely with Progressive Era reformers like Jane Addams. He was succeeded by Dr. Louis L. Mann. Mann would remain the lead rabbi at Sinai until 1962, when he retired. This was the rabbi I would know best as a child and then as a young teenager. By today's standards of megachurches, Sinai was not all that big, but it was large compared to many of the religious organizations of the day. In 1949, Sinai moved into a building at 54th Street and Lake Shore Drive in Hyde Park. I remember the building as being huge. It had an enormous sanctuary where congregants gathered for services—not on Friday evening, as was traditional in Orthodox synagogues, but rather on Sunday morning. The Torah was behind golden doors that opened when the rabbi pressed a button. My sense was, at Sinai, the Torah was revered but not something one accessed on a regular basis to seek religious wisdom. It seemed more like an important relic from the past. While my mother and father attended the service for adults, the kids had a special service in a smaller room followed by religious school.

Rabbi Mann was an imposing figure. A PhD from Yale, he had taught Comparative Ethics before accepting the position at Sinai. In 1963, Rabbi Samuel Karff joined Sinai as the associate rabbi. Seven years later, Rabbi Karff would marry Shaya and me at her parents' home in Lincolnwood. He was a graduate of Harvard who also became deeply involved in social justice issues. In fact, I like to joke that Sinai Temple was politically correct several decades before the term was invented. For example, I remember a sermon that Rabbi Mann gave during the High Holidays on the evils of colonialism. At some point in my religious upbringing, Helen Keller made a visit to Sinai. These liberal, progressive values would have an impact on me as I grew to adulthood. The sermons that Rabbis Mann and Karff gave at Sinai were highly intellectual. As the *Houston Chronicle* observed in Rabbi Karff's obituary, dated August 17–18, 2020, "He was a phenomenal speaker and wove brilliant sermons together by blending biblical scholarship, contemporary literary fiction, current events and film." Although I do not remember the details, I remember a wonderful sermon he gave in which he discussed the spiritual meaning of Saul Bellow's novel, *Henderson the Rain King*, published in 1959.

Reform Judaism (and, one could argue, Judaism in general) has always been concerned about issues of social justice. Perhaps that is a reflection of Jewish theology, which emphasizes the here and now. Judaism's big contribution to the Western world, of course, is the concept that there is only one God who created the universe. In terms of what happens to you after you die, though, mainstream Judaism has always been sketchy. The idea that the soul is eternal is certainly an important tenet of Judaism, but Jews believe what happens to you after you depart this Earth is a mystery. Life is like a candle. It burns slowly at first, and then shines brightly before flickering and going out. Our dear departed loved ones live on in our memories. Compared to Christianity, for example, there isn't much emphasis placed on an eternal life. If you like to watch old movies, there's a humorous discussion of all this in Woody Allen's wonderful movie *Hannah and Her Sisters* (1986). I would not actually be confirmed at Sinai until 1960, after we had left the South Side and moved to Lincolnwood.

**Sinai confirmation class, 1960. Rabbi Mann is on the left, and Rabbi Karff is on the right. I am in the top row in the middle.
(Source: Zucker family photo)**

CHAPTER V
Visiting the Relatives and Family Celebrations

As I have mentioned, my father, Irv, and my mother, Leah, came from very different backgrounds. My father's relatives were Jews from Western Europe. According to immigration records, it appears that my paternal grandfather, Joseph Irving Zucker, arrived in the United States in 1891 around the age of twenty-eight. My maternal grandmother, Sadie Zucker (née Messinger), also came from European Jewish stock. Again, Western European Jews were more inclined to be assimilationists than Eastern European Jews from Poland, et cetera, who were traditionalists.

My mother's relatives were gentiles who came from Austria and the British Isles. Unlike my father's family, the Prides got here early. Through the wonders of Ancestry.com, I have been able to trace the Prides back to the period of the American Revolution. My mother's mother, Anna Rammer, and her relatives also arrived in the New World early. She married my grandfather, Noye Pride, in Antigo, Wisconsin, on January 5, 1907. My father and mother were in that first wave of

American marriages across ethnic, racial, and religious lines. It was not that common back then, but today, it has become a virtual torrent. Even though the Prides and the Rammers arrived in America generations before the Zuckers, in a sense, they remained immigrants, too. That is because from generation to generation, like hundreds of thousands of American families of European descent, the Prides and the Rammers moved farther and farther west until they arrived in northern Wisconsin in the mid-nineteenth century.

On both sides of my family, there were more relatives than you could shake a stick at. This meant that much of the Zucker family time was devoted to visiting relatives.

Visiting the Relatives: The Pride Clan

Most of my mother's relatives remained in northern Wisconsin when I was a child, so we did not see them on a weekly or monthly basis with two exceptions. My mother's brother, Ken Pride, did live close to us in a town in northern Indiana with his wife, Nola, and their two children, my first cousins, Ken Jr. and Connie. We visited back and forth often, seeing them perhaps once every few weeks. Uncle Ken was a combat MP and saw heavy action during WWII. He was a survivor of the Battle of the Bulge, and I believe he suffered from what we refer to today as PTSD, though, in those days, it was called shell shock. Uncle Ken was one of the nicest men I ever met. He loved the outdoors and was an avid fisherman throughout his life. My father helped Uncle Ken get a job in the office at Federated after he returned from the war. Uncle Ken held that position until he retired. Shortly after that, he and Aunt Nola moved to the town of Gaylord in northern Michigan. He passed away in 1993.

Mary Alice Johnson (née Rammer) and her husband, John, were the second exception. The Zucker and the Johnson families visited often, especially during the holidays. My father helped John, who also served in WWII, get a job after the war. He became the superintendent at Chicago White Metal (a die-casting factory), one of my dad's best customers. (During our college years, my brother and I both worked in the shipping room at Chicago White Metal. It was a powerful incentive to continue our education since there are not many places closer to working in hell than a die-casting factory.) John and Mary Alice had two children, Steve and Joyce, who were both considerably younger than my brother and me. I stayed in touch with Joyce occasionally well into my middle age but lost touch with Steve. Mary Alice prepared for us one of the best meals I have ever had. It was sauerbraten, a delicious German dish that was made from deer meat. John and Mary Alice later moved from Chicago to San Antonio, where Shaya and I now reside. They both are buried here at Fort Sam Houston.

**Uncle Ken and Aunt Nola Pride, circa 1950.
(Source: Zucker family photo)**

Each summer, the Zucker family loaded up the family vehicle and headed to northern Wisconsin to visit my mother's extended clan. The trip between Chicago and Antigo took about eight hours since there weren't any interstate highways between the two in the 1950s. The drive, though, was usually pleasant once we escaped Chicago and reached the rolling hills of Wisconsin, dotted with small towns and dairy farms.

We would stop in Clintonville for the most delicious ice cream cones imaginable, made at the local dairy (my favorite was maple nut), and we always drove through the beautiful Menominee Indian reservation where, years later, I would fish for trout on the Wolf River.

Antigo in the 1950s was a town of about 10,000 souls. (It has about the same population today.) Farming was the backbone of the economy then, with some assistance from a growing tourist industry. Most years, we did not bother to stop to visit our relatives in Antigo upon arriving in town, but instead raced ahead the additional seventeen miles on Highway 45 to Summit Lake, where our rustic cabin was waiting for us at King's Resort. ("Rustic" might be a stretch by today's standards.) Our cabin had a kitchen, a living room, a couple of bedrooms, a screened-in porch, and a collection of old furniture. It had a beautiful peek-a-boo view of the lake through the pine and birch trees. The cabin also came with a rowboat (no motor) tied up down at the dock. There was one other resort on the lake (Rasmussen's) and maybe half a dozen summer homes. The lake derives its name from the fact that it is presumably the highest lake in the state, with an elevation of close to 1,800 feet. It was, at least in the 1950s, a true gem. Today, Google Earth shows it is ringed with summer homes. The lake water has a reddish tint to it, and there is one small island toward the far shoreline.

Swimming in the cool waters of Summit Lake was delightful since the lake drops off gradually and has a sandy bottom. There were certainly better fishing lakes around, but Summit Lake was great for kids' fishing. In the 1950s, it was loaded with yellow perch. In the mornings and again in the evenings, my father, my brother, and I would take the boat out, row down the shore a ways, put a worm on our hook, and toss the line out. Within a minute or so, the bobber would go down; we would set the hook; and, after a brief tussle, a perch would be landed. They were rarely big enough to keep. But who cared? The action was nonstop. It was a great way for both of us to begin our lifelong fishing careers. And once in a blue moon, we would get into a school of crappies. Those we kept and ate. Of course, the chore of cleaning the fish fell to my mother.

Fish were not the only quarry we pursued on our childhood vacations to Summit Lake. We also hunted the big green "racing frogs" that populated the Summit Lake Lakeside Cemetery. At the time, the cemetery was overgrown with weeds. Perhaps that's why the frogs liked to hang out there. I thought at the time the frogs were perhaps the reincarnation of the people buried there.

My brother remembered more details about our frog-hunting expeditions than I. We each had a two-pound coffee can (usually Chase & Sanborn) with a coat hanger attached to it so we could carry it at our side. We poked and prodded at the weeds with cottontail stalks, hoping to flush the heavily camouflaged frogs from their hiding places. When we caught one, we would place it in the coffee can and put the top back on. With the two of us beating the bushes, we were able to catch a couple of dozen frogs a day or two before the Zucker family drove back to the Windy City. You may ask what we planned to do with the frogs. Why, my brother planned to sell the slippery amphibians once we got home. He did a lively business peddling most of the frogs to a variety of people: fishermen planning to use the frogs for bait, kids who wanted to own a frog, and so on. Small frogs went for a quarter, medium frogs for fifty cents, and giant frogs for a dollar. Joe remembers one frog that escaped into our basement. I don't know what happened to it.

The tiny hamlet of Summit Lake had a wonderful little ice cream store. In the afternoons, we often hiked to the store to enjoy a delicious ice cream cone. Summit Lake also boasted a rickety baseball field surrounded by trees, where Joe and I practiced hitting and catching. We also loved to play golf at the nearby nine-hole Bass Lake Country Club, which since has expanded to eighteen holes. It was not unusual to find a little frog in the cup after you putted out, and deer frequently scampered across the fairways.

After a round of golf, we would refresh ourselves with a delightful soft drink concoction at the clubhouse. In fact, on several occasions, the Zucker family forsook Summit Lake to rent a cabin on beautiful Bass Lake. In the 1950s, northern Wisconsin was a kid's paradise. I often think about those summer vacations. Perhaps over the span of more than sixty years, I have romanticized them, but I don't think so.

**The Zucker family down at the dock,
Summit Lake, Wisconsin, circa 1955
(Source: Zucker Family Photo)**

On our family sojourns to northern Wisconsin, my poor mother had to beg and plead with us to take a day off from our kids' activities at Summit Lake or Bass Lake to visit relatives in Antigo. Eventually, her pleading would wear us down, and off we would go. Her favorite relative was Uncle Art Rammer, her mother's brother. She often recounted how his ghost stories had scared the hell out of her when she was a girl. Uncle Art was a railroad engineer, following in the footsteps of my grandfather, Noye Pride, who passed away before I was born. In fact, when we were vacationing at Summit Lake, he would blow the locomotive's whistle as the train roared by.

Uncle Art had not always been an engineer, though. As a young man, he had worked for a circus as a tightrope walker and traveled extensively throughout the United States. The story goes that one day he fell off the rope, injured himself, and decided to pursue a different career. I doubt this is why he quit, but it's a good story.

**Uncle Art Rammer in the circus. He is on the left.
(Source: Zucker family photo)**

Those of you who are familiar with Wisconsin know it has its own unique culture made famous by the "cheeseheads." But there is much more to that culture than cheese. In fact, I would rank cheese down on the list behind beer, bratwurst, and the Friday night fish fry at a tavern, restaurant, or supper club—another Wisconsin invention. (In the good old days, perch were the fish of choice at the fish fry, but sadly that has changed because of a huge decline in Lake Michigan's perch population.) Of course, you mustn't forget the Green Bay Packers. I have often joked that before being allowed to take up residency in Wisconsin, you have to pass an entrance exam: you must demonstrate that you know three recipes for preparing bratwurst using beer and have memorized both the starting offensive and defensive lineup for "the Pack."

Wisconsinites know how to have a good time—maybe owing in part to the state's heavy German heritage and in part as a way of compensating for the frequently horrendous weather. The Zucker family spent many wonderful hours on our summer vacations visiting with Uncle Art; his second wife, Dorothy; and their two sons, Michael and James, who were about the same age as my brother and me. Aunt Dorothy made the most delicious rhubarb-strawberry pie. Uncle Art passed away in 1963. We were all sad that he was gone, but that did not stop everybody from having a good time. There were tons of food and libations. Sadly, the only thing missing from the party was Uncle Art.

One year, the Zucker family attended a fake wedding organized by our relatives. My brother remembered this affair better than me. After consulting with him, we recollected there were bride and groom mannequins on the front porch of a cottage somewhere out in the boondocks. I am not sure there was actually a ceremony where the couple was wed in holy matrimony. But that did not matter. The wedding was simply an excuse to have a big party.

When my mother got tired of cooking, our favorite place to eat dinner out was Glenn's High Point, a few minutes drive north on Highway 45 from our cottage. Glenn himself was usually behind the bar serving drinks when we arrived. He always welcomed our family with a hearty "Hello, folks." The dining room was in the back, where you could order a T-bone steak for $1.50 and a whole chicken for $1.25. My brother and I would play the pinball machine while we waited for our food to be cooked. Glenn, an expert fisherman, was always ready to dispense timely tips on where they were biting. Places like Glenn's High Point today are rare.

We also frequented the supper club in Antigo. Supper clubs were big in Wisconsin back in the day, and, in fact, they still are. A wonderful online article by Lindsay Christians in the *Cap Times* entitled "'The Wisconsin Supper Clubs Story' Is a Trip Back in Time" (November 16, 2021) explores the history of Wisconsin supper clubs. Christians interviews Ron Faiola, the author of no fewer than three books on the subject. Interestingly, supper clubs took off in the United States during Prohibition. In order to become a member, you had to pay a small fee, but you were pretty much guaranteed to get in. Today, there are still well over two hundred supper clubs in Wisconsin. I remember dining at one outside Antigo with my family; my mother's best friend from high school, Ruth Walk; and her husband, Bub. Ruth came from one of the wealthiest families in Antigo while my mother came from the poor side of the tracks. They remained good friends throughout their lives, and no trip to Antigo would have been complete without visiting the Walks. Ruth Walk's family owned the hardware store in downtown Antigo. As a high school girl, my mother worked as a soda jerk at the ice cream parlor down the street. The Antigo supper club we dined at was a fancy affair. You got dressed up. If you are wondering what separated the supper club we experienced near Antigo from an ordinary restaurant, the answer is not much. I think they appealed to people, and perhaps still do, because they were considered upscale, and, of course, you had to be a member to dine there. So they were "exclusive." My strongest memory of one of the Zucker family's visits to the Antigo-area supper club was how long it took to get served. After we ordered, I think more than an hour passed before the meal arrived. Several of us had ordered the brook trout, and we all joked they must have had to go out to catch the trout in a local stream prior to preparing them for us. I think Ruth must have taken the photo because she's not in the picture.

The Vanishing World Of My Chicago Childhood

**Dinner at the Antigo Supper Club with Ruth and Bub Walk
(Source: Zucker family photo)**

Although most of my mother's family lived in and around Antigo when I was growing up, the Pride and Rammer clans had already begun to spread out around the state. Some of my mother's aunts lived in Milwaukee—only about ninety miles north of Chicago, so it wasn't too hard to visit them. We were particularly close to the Eastwood family who lived in Stevens Point, which is located in central Wisconsin. We often stopped by to visit them, either on our way to Antigo or on the way home. Fritz and Gretchen had two children, a boy and a girl. Gretchen was related to my mother, but don't ask me how. Tragically, their son, Bill, was diagnosed as a child with a debilitating nerve disorder (probably infantile paralysis). I still remember when the Eastwoods came to visit us one summer in Chicago, and Billy was falling down frequently as we played. When I asked my mother why this was happening, she said he had a serious illness, and it was only going to get worse. Billy died at the age of sixteen. We remained close to their daughter, Susan, for many years but finally lost touch with her. Today, I am no longer in any meaningful contact with my Wisconsin relatives.

Benny the Beagle: A Boy's Best Friend

As one of our visits to the Eastwoods was drawing to a close, we were standing out in front of their house getting ready to depart for Chicago when we noticed the next-door neighbor's house was for sale. We asked why the house was on the market. Fritz informed us his neighbor had passed away. We said we were sorry to learn the sad news, but Fritz's reply was there was nothing to be sad about. He said, "He had a good life. He had three good dogs." I have to admit, although the Zucker family enjoyed visiting our relatives during our vacations to beautiful northern Wisconsin, we did consider ourselves to be city slickers and our Wisconsin relatives to be something of country bumpkins. So it struck us at the time as somewhat odd and humorous that Fritz would think someone had a good life because he had three good dogs. Funny how life teaches you lessons along the way. The wisdom of what Fritz said that day has resonated with me through my senior years. I, too, have had three good dogs, and I consider them to be among the major blessings of my life.

My first dog was Benny the Beagle. Actually, his pedigree name was Benton's Benjamin. (He was born in Benton, Illinois.) How did we acquire Benny? In the way that countless families have wound up with their pet dogs. We went out for a family ride on a Sunday afternoon. Either before we got in the car or shortly thereafter, we decided we would just look at some puppies. You know how that goes.

We stopped at a kennel to see what puppies they had for sale. Inside was a pen holding several baby beagles. Now, puppies are generally outrageously cute, but beagle puppies are among the most adorable. There were three or four in the pen, and they were all eager to be adopted, jumping up and down, barking, and wagging their tails. But one puppy, although friendly, was just a little more reserved than the others. That is the one we decided to buy. I think my dad paid about thirty-five dollars for Benny, and the kennel owner threw in a leather leash and collar for free. How exciting! By the time we got home, Benny had chewed his leather leash in half. Oh well.

Benny was the best childhood pal a boy could ever have. Of course, he was not just my dog. We all loved him. If you know anything about beagles, then you know they are hunting dogs and must be kept on a leash. They will go wherever their nose leads them. That means they run away whenever the chance presents itself. And Benny was no exception.

The times he ran away are too numerous to recount. Once when we were vacationing at Bass Lake, Benny escaped from our cottage. We were panic stricken. Which way did he go? How long had he been gone? I took off down a path looking for him. After a few minutes, I saw him running toward me. He did not stop when he saw me but zipped right on past, heading for the cottage. What could have caused him to reverse course? We discovered his nose was swollen: a bee had stung him.

Beagles are very smart, but they are also extremely stubborn. They have a mind of their own. Benny (like most dogs) was a superb beggar for table scraps. It was nearly impossible to resist those big sad brown eyes. One day, I made a beggar's license for him, hung it around his neck, and put him on the front porch to "beg." He loved popsicles and usually got a blueberry-flavored one for his birthday treat. Benny was also a creature of habit. He had a definite routine: a time to eat, a time to go for a walk, and a time to snooze. Benny loved to sleep on the couch in our living room. In order to accommodate him, my mother would spread a small sheet on the couch when it was his bedtime.

One Saturday evening, it was my parents' turn to host their gin rummy club. This was a big affair: maybe a dozen or more couples all playing gin in our house. After the card playing was over around ten pm, it was time for food and drinks. The party generally lasted until close to midnight. As the evening wore on, Benny grew more and more forlorn. Sometime around eleven p.m., my mother saw him walking from the kitchen where the sheet was kept to the living room with the sheet in his mouth. He was announcing to everyone that it was well past his bedtime, and they all needed go home.

Benny lived long past my years on the South Side. When we moved to Lincolnwood in 1960, Benny, of course, went with us. He lived long enough for my future wife to get to know him. In fact, he had a habit of interfering with our smooching on the couch in the family room when we were dating. He wanted attention.

I shall not dwell on my other two good dogs since both lived with my wife and me long after the time frame of this story. Both were Old English sheepdogs. We purchased the first of the two, Sophie, from a breeder in the Chicago area while living in Champaign, Illinois. The second was Sarie, whom we purchased from Sue and Frank Rhia, our good friends, while living in Austin, Texas. *Requiescat in pace*, Benny, Sophie, and Sarie.

**Benny the Beagle and Me in the Backyard, circa 1957.
(Source: Zucker Family Photo)**

Visiting the Relatives: The Zucker Clan

As I mentioned earlier, the Zuckers were Western European Jews who came from countries like Germany and Austria. I never knew either of my paternal grandparents, both of whom passed away before I was born. My grandfather, Joseph Irving Zucker, died on the operating table when my father was a small child; my grandmother, Sadie Zucker, passed away in the 1930s, well before I was born. My father's sister and brother both tragically died in their youth. His sister caught fire and burned to death as a teenager while burning the garbage on a windy day in the alley behind their residence. His brother died of tuberculosis as a young man. So, in terms of immediate family members and my father's side of the family, we were out of luck. Nonetheless, in my childhood, there were plenty of Zucker relatives to visit in the Chicago area.

Two of our favorites were Jay and June Messinger. Jay was related to my grandmother Sadie's side of the family and came from educated Western European Jews. The Starkmans, June's immediate relatives, came from Eastern European Jewish stock. Jay was a graduate of the prestigious University of Chicago Law School and was already practicing law when I was growing up. Jay and June visited us frequently at our home at 8610 Rhodes Avenue, and we often visited them in their apartment on the South Side. What I liked most about Jay was that he enjoyed having fun. During one visit, I remember Jay, my brother, and I had a lively game of marbles in our next-door neighbor's yard. At some point, Mrs. D or her boyfriend chased us away. Why we decided to play marbles in the neighbor's yard instead of our own, I have never been able to figure out.

Unlike many of our relationships with my father's family, which did not last beyond my childhood years, the Zuckers' relationship with Jay and June Messinger was enduring. Years later, when we moved to Lincolnwood, Jay and June moved to nearby Skokie. They had two children: Lee, their daughter, and Allen, their son. The two families continued to visit back and forth during our suburban years. Jay was also a passionate Cubs fan, so we always had the Cubs' misfortunes to commiserate about. Jay and June were also among the very early collectors of my brother's artwork. Years ago, the Messinger family donated one of Joe's early paintings to the Art Institute of Chicago. Sadly, Jay and June are now both deceased.

We also visited with the Barnet family, who lived in a big apartment on Lake Shore Drive in Chicago. The Barnets were cousins of my father, but I am not sure how they were related. Mark Barnet was also an attorney. He loved to sail in his big yacht on Lake Michigan. My brother and I played with their two daughters when we went to visit.

My memory of my father's other relatives in Chicago is foggy. That is because they were mostly very old—aunts and uncles and some cousins. I do remember visiting Aunt Hannah on the weekends, for example, but I do not recall much about her except she seemed somewhat strange to my brother and me. I do remember my father saying Aunt Hannah had advised him after he made a ton of money selling real estate in the late 1920s or early 1930s to hide the money under his mattress. Of course, he did not listen to her, and when the Great Depression struck, he lost it all.

Though my dad could be extremely charming, there was another, darker side to him. He had a terrible temper and frequently lashed out at my brother and me. I remember more than one occasion when I crawled under my bed to escape my father's wrath as he chased my brother and me around the house with a strap. (I can't imagine what the two of us could have been doing to cause such a scene.) Also, he and my mother had huge arguments. I have no idea what these arguments were about. I can only speculate they may have had something to do with my father's penchant for playing the ponies at the racetrack. Maybe he was losing too much money. Or it could have been that my mother grew weary of covering for him when the office of Federated Metals where he worked called looking for him when he was at the racetrack. Remember, this was before cell phones, so the office did not have any way of contacting Irv unless he called in. His bad temper on occasion boiled over into his work. I remember my mother being terrified because he had had an altercation with a colleague in the parking lot at Federated Metals. Apparently, some punches were exchanged. In fact, his explosive temper was so bad that he became famous in the neighborhood for screaming and yelling.

I often reflect on how the many family tragedies my father experienced as a child and young man must have affected him. His explosive temper, I believe, was a consequence of experiencing them. Irv Zucker passed away in his early eighties, after moving to Florida with his second wife. The funeral was held in Chicago in the dead of winter. A rabbi was hired to officiate at my father's internment. The rabbi, who had never met my dad, talked to many relatives and friends in order to get a sense of what he was like before officiating at the funeral. I do not remember the rabbi's exact opening comments, but they were something to the effect of "Irv Zucker was not an easy man to get along with." People nodded. But then the rabbi went on to explain that, overall, he had been a good father and husband and had helped many people during his life. Again, the gathering nodded their heads in agreement.

My mother had, for many years, been taking care of her invalid mother and partially disabled father. I believe perhaps she was attracted to Irv in part because he gave her someone to care for after her parents were gone. My mother definitely had a caregiver's personality. She was always dispensing advice to people who were sick, even when she was ill herself. Leah Zucker tragically passed away from cancer during my sophomore year at the University of Wisconsin. My father, brother, and I were grief stricken beyond comprehension at her untimely death. Unlike my troubled father, who could be difficult, Leah was adored by everyone who knew her. Even though she had converted to Judaism, my brother, a few close relatives, and I often referred to her as "Saint Leah" after she had departed this Earth.

Family Holidays and Celebrations

Holidays, of course, were a big deal then as they are now. Although my mother converted to Judaism after she married my dad, like a lot of American families from mixed religious backgrounds, we celebrated both Jewish and Christian holidays. One of my favorite sayings is "If they give gifts, I celebrate it." So, yes, we had a Christmas tree (a.k.a. Hanukkah bush) in the living room. The big joke was what we were going to do if the rabbi came to visit.

My brother and I grew up believing in Santa Claus just like our Christian neighbors. In fact, one year when I was about six or seven years old, I was certain I heard Santa and his reindeer land on our roof. My brother, who was four years older than I, wasn't so sure. What kind of presents did we get for Hanukkah? Well, this holiday in our family was not that important when it came to gifts. In fact, I don't remember any presents I received. The tradition over the decades for Jewish families, though, has been to give practical gifts. Take socks, for example. When I had children of my own, giving socks for Hanukkah became a kind of humorous tradition after *Saturday Night Live*'s hilarious skit on the subject aired many years ago. In the skit, Santa Claus becomes ill on Christmas Eve and calls Hanukkah Harry, played by Jon Lovitz, to ask Harry to substitute for him. Hanukkah Harry says, "Why, sure," and loads up his cart, which is pulled through the air by several braying donkeys, with loads of gifts for the gentile children. The problem is that the gifts are all socks. The gentile kids are mightily disappointed on Christmas morning when they discover they received a whole bunch of socks instead of the bright shiny toys they were expecting. In recent decades, though, Hanukkah has been "upgraded" among Jewish families to compete with Christmas.

What sort of gifts did my brother and I find under the tree on Christmas morning? Well, of course, there would have been clothes—perhaps shirts, pajamas, sweaters, et cetera. But those are gifts children look at for a minute or two and say, "Gee, thanks, Mom and Dad." Since it has been more than sixty years since I opened a Christmas present at 8610 Rhodes Avenue, it is difficult to remember. And it is also true that I would have received the same kinds of presents for birthdays and other holidays. So what were they? Surprisingly, one of my favorite presents was a book containing all sorts of different subjects. It had corny jokes, some of which I still remember today; information about sports teams; and many other interesting topics. My brother and I liked to collect beautifully decorated toy soldiers made out of lead, so I am sure we received some of those. We would have received board games such as Monopoly or Clue; additions to our Lionel train set and village, which occupied the ping-pong table down in the basement during the holiday season; and, of course, sporting goods of all kinds. One of my favorite gifts was a microscope. I spent countless hours as a child examining the wonders of salt crystals and various other minerals.

The major difference between the presents Joe and I received and the presents my grandchildren receive lies in the fact that electronic toys had not been invented during my childhood. So there were no video games, cell phones, and so on. And I don't remember receiving plastic toys, either. I am convinced that plastic toys are the curse of modern parenting. For many years, my grandchildren received tons of them. Each plastic toy, which may contain dozens if not hundreds of parts, has to be assembled. So Dad or Mom spends an hour or so trying to figure out how to put the darn thing together. Once it has been put together, the kids play with it for a few hours, and then the toy winds up cluttering the house. More often than not, pieces fall off the toy and cannot be found, or they break. Eventually, the toy winds up in a container somewhere before being hauled off to the Goodwill store.

When it was time to take down the Christmas trees, most people in our neighborhood would drag them out into the alley where they would be picked up by the city of Chicago's garbage trucks. The goal of the boys in the neighborhood was to collect as many trees as possible before the garbage truck got to them. We would then store them in someone's backyard until they had thoroughly dried out. When the big day came, we would then haul them to a vacant lot where they would be ignited, creating a huge bonfire. Was this dangerous? I am sure it was. I don't remember whether or not there was adult supervision.

Birthdays

Of course, birthdays were a big deal for the children in our neighborhood. My pals would be invited to my party, which usually featured a delicious birthday cake baked by my mother, with sloppy Joes, potato chips, and all the fixings for the main dish. I wish I had some photos of the whole gang assembled, but over time, they all disappeared. What I do have are lots of birthday photos of me from when I was a relatively small child. Of course, the kids brought presents. We must have played games as part of my birthday celebration, but I have forgotten what many of them were. I asked my wife what games she played at her birthday parties. She immediately replied, "Pin the Tail on the Donkey." That jogged my memory; we played that one, too. In this game, a picture of a donkey missing a tail is placed on the wall. The contestants are blindfolded, spun around a few times, and then asked to pin the tail on the donkey. The contestant who comes closest wins the game and is awarded a prize. It's very entertaining. I suppose one major difference between birthday celebrations of middle-class kids then as opposed to now is that, back in the day, parents did not bring in outside entertainment, nor were we taken to any amusement establishments. So birthday parties for middle-class kids were generally a lot less expensive than they are today.

The Fourth of July

The most exciting holiday for my brother and me was the Fourth of July. The excitement began weeks if not months before when we received several catalogs in the mail advertising fireworks for sale. The big issue was what package to go with. Should we opt for the fifteen-dollar "all noise" fireworks or split our money between firecrackers and the "non-noise" selection, which included Roman candles, snakes, sparklers, and other assorted goodies. Of course, being boys, our final selection was heavily weighted toward fireworks that exploded. Always popular were the loud (and dangerous) "Black Cats." But the small "lady fingers" that exploded one after another were also among our favorites. A check would be placed in the mail, and a few weeks later, the package would arrive. As a child, I cannot remember ever going to an organized Fourth of July fireworks show. We did it all ourselves. Of course, the parents helped put together the shows, which took place in one of our vacant fields. But a lot of the activity children engaged in was unsupervised. How my brother and I and our neighborhood pals survived without losing an eye or a finger is totally beyond me.

One year, Calvin and Jeff's dad, Mr. E., decided he would instruct the neighborhood kids in the proper use of fireworks by putting on a safety demonstration. Mr. E. worked for the telephone company and undoubtedly had some experience with safety on the job. So a bunch of us assembled in the the family's backyard to watch the demonstration. Mr. E. decided to show us how to safely launch bottle rockets. For the uninitiated, bottle rockets are little missiles you put in a milk bottle (remember those?), and then you light the fuse with a match. Once ignited, they make a loud noise and shoot perhaps twenty feet into the air.

Mr. E. lit up a cigarette before putting a bunch of the little rockets in about half a dozen bottles. As you may know, smoking cigarettes was quite popular in the 1950s. In fact, just about all adults did. As he was addressing his young charges, he decided to put down the cigarette on the wooden ledge of the fence directly behind him. With his back to the fence, he could not see his cigarette roll off the ledge and land in one of the bottles. You can probably guess what happened next. With a loud boom, several of the rockets ignited and took off for the sky above us, startling him. He laughed and said that was *not* how to do it. That was the end of the demonstration. Maybe you had to be there. But I still chuckle every time I think of his safety demonstration gone awry.

Perhaps the most dangerous thing we did was put a Black Cat firecracker in a metal tube about six feet long. We then inserted a marble into the barrel of the tube and lit the fuse on the firecracker. When the firecracker exploded, the marble exited the tube at a high velocity. How high? Suffice it to say that the marbles frequently went through the sides of the metal garbage cans in the alley where the shenanigans took place.

CHAPTER VI

Out on the Town, Discovering Girls, and a Changing Culture

Of course, there were plenty of things for the Zucker family to do outside the immediate neighborhood in which we lived. We explored Chicago extensively. Toward the end of my years at 8610 Rhodes Avenue, I began another kind of exploration. I discovered girls at a time when American teenage culture was going through a profound transformation.

A Day at Wrigley Field

**Chicago Cubs Baseball Game at Wrigley Field, 1950s
(With permission oft he Chicago Historical Museum)**

One of the favorite pastimes for the three menfolk in the Zucker family during the summer was to take in a Chicago Cubs baseball game. I have not mentioned that my father worked for the Chicago Cubs sometime in the 1920s and possibly into the 1930s. Irv also had worked for his uncle Sam Messinger, who owned a string of bakeries in Chicago during the 1930s. When I would ask my dad what his duties were for Uncle Sam, he would reply that he was "the taster."

Irv Zucker was not a scholar by any stretch of the imagination. My brother and I once found one of his report cards from Tuley High School in the garage after we moved to Lincolnwood. It was filled with

Cs and Ds. My father had a self-deprecating sense of humor—he loved to tell a story on himself. His high school graduation play had been about the discovery of the New World. His part in the play consisted of one line: "Land ho." He forgot it. Irv was no dummy, though. He was a super salesman and a good businessman. What he may have lacked in academic achievement, he more than made up for it with his business talents.

How did my father get his job working for the Cubs? Not through the traditional means of sending in a résumé and then being selected for the job after an interview. No. Instead, according to the story he told many times when I was growing up, he got his job after being caught trying to sneak into the ballpark. You might ask, "How was this possible?" Well, the Wrigley Field of the 1920s was not the brick fortress it is today. In any case, instead of booting my dad out of the park or turning him over to the authorities, the man who caught my dad said, "Hey, kid, if you want to see the game, why don't you take tickets? We need ticket takers."

So my father started out taking tickets. From that humble position, he worked his way up into the front office, where he worked for several years (how many exactly, I do not know). During one series when the Cubs were playing the Saint Louis Cardinals (the Cubs' archrivals), he was invited to sit on the bench with the team. This was a big deal back then as it would be now. His career with the Cubs came to a rather abrupt end, however, when he was passed over for the job of traveling secretary for the ball club. It's the traveling secretary's duties, in part, to ride herd on the ballplayers when the team is on the road. The top management of the Cubs thought my dad looked too young, so the position went to someone else who looked older. My father quit in a huff. Still, having any connection with the Cubs is a huge deal in Chicago. My cousin Jay Messinger often told my brother and me he thought my dad had landed his salesman job with Federated Metals because he had worked for the Cubs.

Several times each summer, the three Zucker men (and sometimes my mother, too) would make the trip from the South Side of Chicago to Wrigley Field, located on the city's near North Side. In those days, we could find a parking spot on the street maybe three or four blocks from the ballpark. More often than not, we walked to the pass gate where people who had connections could get into the park for free. Although this was some twenty years or more after he had worked for the Cubs, the person working the pass gate almost always knew my dad, so we would be waved on through. Now, you may think it was a big deal to get into a Cubs game for free, but please remember, this was the 1950s. The Cubs had one of the worst teams in the National League, if not all of baseball. Their pitching staff was more notorious for its nightclub romps on Rush Street than for its skills on the pitching mound. The position players weren't any better. So, on a summer weekday, maybe five thousand to ten thousand fans would be in attendance. And, of course, all these games were played during the day since Wrigley Field had no lights.

There was definitely a downside, though, to getting into the park for free. We had to arrive early at the pass gate. So, after entering the park, we would find vacant seats in the grandstand, maybe around eleven-thirty a.m. We would watch batting practice, pencil the starting lineup into the scorecard, read the *Chicago Sun-Times*, and perhaps munch on a sandwich my mother had prepared. The only problem was, after we had done all these things, the umpire had not yet hollered, "Play ball!" Sometimes, though, my father purchased grandstand tickets, and we could arrive later. If memory serves, grandstand tickets went for $1.50, and I think you could land a seat in the bleachers for about a buck. Today, a ticket to see the Cubs in the reserved grandstands will cost you a hundred dollars or more. We often also chose to sit in the right or left field bleachers. The famous Cubs "bleacher bums" made the game entertaining even when the Cubs were taking a shellacking by heckling the opposing team's right or left fielder—especially after they made an error. The bleacher bums are still alive and kicking today.

How terrible were the Cubs in the 1950s? Well, I could bore you to tears with a lot of statistics. In this era, there were eight baseball teams in the National League. It was—and still is—a tradition at Wrigley Field to fly the pennants of the teams above the scoreboard in center field in the order of their standings. Suffice it to say, when we attended a game anytime in July or August, the Cubs pennant would be flying near or at the bottom of the eight. When the Milwaukee Braves came to town with their ace pitcher, Warren Spahn, and their home run–hitting slugger, Eddie Mathews, you could expect the Cubbies to take a drubbing. Even worse was when the Cubs hosted the Brooklyn Dodgers with their murderous lineup and stellar pitching staff.

At least things got more interesting when the Cubs brought up Ernie Banks, their first African American player, from the minors in 1953. "Mr. Cub" would thrill us for many years with his patented line-drive home runs into the left field bleachers. By the way, the fact that we lived on the South Side meant we were in closer proximity to Chicago's other Major League Baseball team, the White Sox. Though we took in many more Cub games than Sox contests, we often journeyed to Comiskey Park. The White Sox at least had a decent team, with star players like Minnie Minoso, Nellie Fox, Sherman Loller, and Billy Pearce. Most of our neighborhood pals like the M. Boys were White Sox fans.

The Trip to Evanston for a Northwestern Basketball Game

Once a year, my father would purchase tickets for the whole family to attend a Northwestern University basketball game. We would pile into the family sedan and make the forty-five minutes drive from the South Side of Chicago to watch the Wildcats play one of their Big Ten rivals. As you may know, for many decades, Northwestern remained the only private university in the Big Ten after the University of Chicago dropped out in the early twentieth century. With Northwestern's high academic standards, its basketball teams were doomed to having trouble competing in the Big Ten. The construction of the McGaw Memorial

Hall, in which today's Welsh-Ryan Arena is located, was completed in 1952. So the Zucker family would have watched most of the games in a brand-new facility. As I write, that facility has finally been replaced by a new one. The NU hoops teams in the 1950s were at least competitive—generally speaking—and each year, they had some terrific players. I still remember many of them.

Thanks to the Northwestern men's basketball archives online, I can go back in time and look at the rosters and the team's results in a given year. For example, in 1954, the Wildcats' star player was Frank Ehmann, who averaged 19.5 points per game—good enough for seventh place in the Big Ten. That year, Northwestern finished fifth in the league with a 6–8 conference record—one of their better finishes. I remember watching "Whitey" Ehmann play. The game I remember best, though, came somewhat late in the Zucker treks to see Northwestern play. It was the 1960–1961 season. Northwestern was hosting the undefeated Ohio State Buckeyes, and we had tickets. All week, the Chicago sports reporters were hyping the game. Could the underdog Wildcats, who were not all that bad, upset the mighty Buckeyes? This was a phenomenal Buckeye team that starred Jerry Lucas at center, John Havlicek at forward, and Mel Nowell at guard. Bobby Knight, who would became a legendary coach at Indiana, was a reserve guard. We anxiously awaited the tip-off between Lucas and Northwestern's center, "Big Bill" Woislaw.

Finally the moment came. The Buckeyes won the jump ball. A guard passed the ball to Lucas, who tossed in a beautiful hook shot from around the free throw line. A gasp went up from the crowd. The rout was on. I don't remember the final score. We probably left early. Ohio State would go on to be undefeated that season, winning the national championship. My brother and I would continue to attend Wildcat basketball games—and also some football games—as young men. We continued throughout our adulthood to watch NU sports on TV. Sadly, now that he is deceased, I do not have another passionate Northwestern fan to talk to about the trials and tribulations of the university's athletic teams.

Riverview: The World's Largest Amusement Park

**A roller coaster at Riverview Park.
(With permission of the Chicago Historical Museum)**

Amusement parks were big in the 1950s, just as they are today. And when I was growing up, Chicago had an amusement park that billed itself as the world's largest. Riverview Park opened in July 1904 as the German Sharpshooter Park, owned by the Schmidt family, at the intersection of Belmont and Western Avenues on the city's near North Side. According to an online article on Riverview in the Chicago Time Machine, women and children complained they had nothing to do while the men shot their guns, so two years later, the owners commissioned a spectacular handcrafted carousel with seventy horses. In 1905, the Schmidts bought fifty more acres and began to expand the number of rides and attractions. The Riverview I remember as a child and later as a young adult was a special place, though quite different from the Disney parks, Seven Flags over Texas, and the other amusement parks of today.

It was, well, quirkier. In addition, to a large number of hair-rising rides, there was also a fun house and a freak show.

The most spectacular of the many roller coaster rides was "The Bobs." It was billed as the world's fastest roller coaster and actually hit a top speed of more than sixty miles per hour. The two-and-a-half-minute ride with its horrific abrupt eighty-five-foot drop and steeply banked turns left people breathless. The Bobs carried an estimated twelve hundred passengers per hour and drew some seven hundred thousand riders each season. Did I ever have the nerve to tackle the Bobs? Why, of course! To tell you the truth, I don't remember. I like to think I did. Maybe I opted for one of the less scary roller coaster rides.

Another ride I remember well was "The Rotor." I know I was too much of a chicken to try this one. It was a spinning contraption where the floor dropped out from under the people who were held to the wall by centrifugal force. I still remember watching them and hearing their screams. "Pair-O-Chutes" was another scary one. People were lifted to the top of a very tall tower before dropping in carts attached to parachutes. It was the first free-fall parachute ride ever constructed. Okay, so I never went on Pair-O-Chutes, either. Maybe it was because the parachutes had a nasty habit of getting stuck at the top. I know I read more than one article in the Chicago newspapers about patrons getting stranded—sometimes for several hours. Of course, there were tamer rides like the Ferris wheel, a miniature train, and the aforementioned carousel. For the romantically inclined teenagers and adults, there was the "Tunnel of Love." Before we were married, Shaya and I went on several dates to Riverview. And, of course, we could not depart without a trip through the Tunnel of Love.

But there was a darker side to Riverview. A number of attractions were designed to scare and amaze you. One of my favorites was a classic fun house, "Aladdin's Castle." It was filled with distorted mirrors, a maze of screen doors, floors with twirling disks, and a machine that blew a blast of air from the floor that could blow an unsuspecting woman's skirt up over her head. Then there was the freak show: human beings on display for their abnormalities. A barker stood out front, luring customers into the show. There were a mule-faced woman, a sword swallower, and many others. There was also a dunking tank where white patrons tossed balls at a target with black men sitting on a seat above a tank of water. If the ball hit the target, the man got dunked in the water. Pressure from the NAACP caused this attraction to close in the 1960s.

Unfortunately, by the mid-1960s, Riverview was going into a tailspin for a variety of reasons. It closed its doors in 1967. Chicagoans of many generations have a warm spot in their hearts for Riverview, including me. What's there today? According to an article in Wikipedia, the former grounds are now home to the Riverview Plaza shopping center, the Chicago Police Area 3 Detective Division, DePaul College Prep School, a manufacturing company, and Richard Clark Park, part of the Chicago Park District. The south end of the park has a wooded area where many of the Riverview Park foundations are still visible and is currently used as a bicycle dirt jump track. The Riverview Carousel continues to operate at Six Flags over Georgia—the only ride to be saved. (If you would like to know more about Riverview, there's a wonderful PBS documentary online: *Chicago Stories—Riverview*, hosted by WTTW's John Callaway.)

Going to the Movie Theaters

We had two movie theaters in our neighborhood. The first was the Rhodes Theatre, located on South Rhodes Avenue and East 79th Street, not more than a mile or so from our house. The second was the Avalon Theater, located somewhat farther away from our home but also on 79th Street. The Rhodes Theatre has been demolished; the Avalon still stands today but is closed.

Scary Science Fiction Movies

Many of the flicks from my childhood that stand out in my memory were scary science fiction movies. I saw several of them for the first time, either at the Rhodes or the Avalon; others, I may have viewed for the first time on TV. I believe science fiction flicks were big in America in the 1950s for two reasons. The first was the development of the atomic bomb that the United States dropped on Hiroshima and on Nagasaki in August 1945. The A-bomb was followed by the invention of the even more terrifying H-bomb. For the first time in history, mankind had to face the possibility that all human life on Earth might be extinguished by a nuclear holocaust. The second was the fear of communism. People might not be who they seemed. Your next-door neighbor who seemed like a pleasant enough chap could secretly be a communist agent working to overthrow the government of the United States. These movies subliminally reflected the fears of the American population in that era. A few of the movies that terrified me the most were *It Came from Outer Space* (1953 in 3D), based on a story by the acclaimed science fiction writer Ray Bradbury; *The Invasion of the Body Snatchers* (1956), adapted from a novel by Jack Finney; and *Them!* (1954), one of the first 1950s nuclear monster movies and the first big film to use insects as monsters.

Cartoons

My brother and I looked forward excitedly to getting off school for George Washington's Birthday (now rebranded as President's Day). Since 1879, Washington's Birthday had been an official federal holiday, so we were sprung from Dixon Elementary School for the day. Nowadays, Presidents' Day is just another in a long list of school holidays for children, so I don't detect a lot of excitement from my grandkids about it. But for brother Joe and me it was a big deal because the local movie theaters ran a special program: they showed twenty-five cartoons! Sometime in the early afternoon, my dad would drop the two of us off at the Rhodes Theatre. (My poor wife has heard the following story innumerable times.) One year when I must have been seven or eight, when the cartoons started, I became so excited I threw my cap up into the air, but when it came down, I never found it. Gone. I worried what my parents would say about me losing my cap. But my memory is that they did not make a big deal out of it. Today, it would be hard to explain to my grandchildren why going to the movie theater to see several hours of Bugs Bunny, Donald Duck, Popeye, Woody the Woodpecker, Tom and Jerry, and many others would be so exciting. I am sure we enjoyed popcorn and soda pops as we watched the program. When the cartoons were over, we would wait outside for my dad to pick us up for the ride home. Kids in the third decade of the twenty-first century have the opportunity to watch hundreds of different animated programs on a variety of different media sources twenty-four hours a day. Even after the Zucker family purchased its first TV, cartoon programs were not always available.

Going Out for Dinner

Going out for dinner was popular back then, as it is now. Of course, my mother and father went out to dinner on their own, but often, it was a family affair. In the 1950s, the trend was for upwardly mobile middle-class families to patronize "fancy" restaurants, and the Zucker family was no exception. My dad and mom both got dressed up, and, to the extent that boys get dressed up, Joe and I did, too. The big deal back then was the many-course meal, starting with appetizers, followed by a salad, main course, and then dessert. Lazy Susans were popular back then, so I am sure many of our meals featured those, too. What do I remember ordering? Geez. That's a tough one. As a small child, I was a picky eater, but as time went by, my palate expanded. One thing I do remember is that I often ordered the tomato cocktail as my appetizer. I still wonder why I ordered tomato juice, which I am sure came right out of a can, but I liked it. Roast beef, steaks, and chicken were popular entrée dishes.

Our neighborhood did not have any fancy restaurants, but that wasn't a problem. My father liked to drive, and Chicago was much easier to get around in those days than it is now. One of the family favorites was Barney's Market Club. According to a nice article by Rick Kogan published in the *Chicago Tribune* (January 24, 2011) entitled "Yes Sir,

Senator," this restaurant was noted for its steaks, its serious drinks, and its famous slogan, which everyone assumed was born of the frequent patronage by local politicians. (After inhabiting several other locations around the city, it moved to Halsted and Polk Streets, where it remained popular for more than six decades.) Though many elected officials, mobsters, businessmen, cops, and others on their way to and from events at the Chicago Stadium were known to drop in, Kogan states that it was the owner Barney Kessel's inability to remember anyone's name that gave birth to the slogan. He apparently called almost everyone senator. Did we ever see any politicians there? Not that I remember, though I doubt any of us would have recognized one anyway, unless perhaps it had been Mayor Richard J. Daley. Silly as it sounds, I remember the Zucker family being excited by dining at a restaurant that entertained such famous customers. And the food was pretty good, too.

My brother reminded me of another family favorite I had forgotten. Mickelberry's Log Cabin Restaurant was located at 2300 West 95th Street, not more than five miles from our house on Rhodes Avenue. The Digital Research Library of Illinois History Journal (Wednesday, October 2, 2019) has a wonderful history of Mickelberry's by Neil Gale, PhD. The original restaurant opened in 1933 and was modeled after the Mickelberry ancestral plantation home in Spaulding County, Georgia. Campbell Wallace Mickelberry, his brother Charles, and Jay Adler were the original partners. Adler was a horse lover, a Civil War buff, an authority on Indian history, and an antique collector. The restaurant served dishes like buckwheat pancakes, freshly made sausages, homemade breads, and southern fried chicken and, on Thanksgiving, roast tom turkey for $2.75. The article has a reproduction of the Mickelberry's Thanksgiving menu for 1960. The list of appetizers was extensive, starting out with my favorite, "Chilled Tomato Juice." For thirty-five cents extra, a patron could order a "Fresh Shrimp Cocktail." The restaurant was one of several that were mysteriously bombed in Chicago during the summer of 1964. It reopened but went out of business for good three years later.

I learned from my wife that her family was doing much the same thing on the north side of Chicago in the 1950s. One of her family's favorite restaurants was Di Leo's, located at 5700 North Central Avenue. It was a fancy Italian restaurant that featured a relish tray. In fact, my wife and I had dinner there with her parents many times both before and after we were married. Many Chicagoans even today have fond memories of Di Leo's. But, you may ask what, about all the other cuisine Chicago is famous for? Well, many of those places I experienced later in my life after I became a young adult: Uno's Pizzeria in downtown Chicago; Hackney's on Harms Road in Glencoe, where my wife and I went on our first date; Mustard's Last Stand in Evanston; and too many others to mention here.

Shopping

When I was growing up, shopping was a major activity for the Zucker family as it is for most families today. We shopped for food at the local grocery store, but, of course, we also shopped for a wide variety of consumer items, including clothing, furniture and decorations for the home, appliances, automobiles, sporting goods, and more.

For centuries, Jews in the Old Country were restricted from entering most professions because of discriminatory legislation. One thing Jews were allowed to do, however, was sell merchandise. So, throughout Europe, they were heavily involved in selling all manner of items in small shops and by peddling goods door to door. When Jews immigrated to the United States in huge numbers in the late nineteenth and early twentieth centuries, they brought this tradition with them. The Chicago I grew up in the 1950s had hundreds of smaller stores with Jewish proprietors. Many of these stores were concentrated in two areas: Roosevelt Road and Maxwell Street.

When it came to purchasing clothing, my father would often take my brother and me to shop at stores located on Roosevelt Road. One of his favorites was Independent Clothing, which occupied the second floor of a large building. But not everyone could enter Independent

Clothing. Oh no. You had to know someone. Why was this? Because Independent Clothing was a wholesale establishment, so the prices were rock-bottom cheap. When it came to buying something, my father loved to get a deal, and this store was the mecca of deals on clothing.

After we were buzzed through the door, we walked up the stairs to the second floor, and entered a large room that was filled with all manner of men's clothing: shirts, pants, sweaters, sports coats, suits—you name it. Over the years, much, though not all, of my clothing came from this store. Although some of the clothes were nice, a lot of them were, well, not so great. That's why they were so cheap. Our trips to Independent Clothing lasted well beyond my childhood. A blue sports coat I wore on my honeymoon came from the store.

A second store we visited on Roosevelt Road carried shoes (also wholesale). They had name brands from that era such as Florsheim, but a lot of shoes the store sold were seconds: that is, they had a defect of some kind. Usually, the defect was small—not even noticeable. But one pair of shoes my dad purchased for me had defective dye. When I wore them in the rain for the first time, the dye ran off them. A third store we visited was really was a throwback to the Old World. It mainly sold men's underwear. The underwear, though, was not out on display where you could see it. Instead, it was all behind the counter. So you would tell the proprietor what you wanted—for example, boy's underwear, six medium—and he would get it for you. To my knowledge, stores like this simply do not exist anymore in the United States.

Aerial view of Maxwell Street, 1945
(With permission of the Chicago History Museum)

Roosevelt Road, though, was a step up from Maxwell Street, a place that was filled with small shops selling everything. There were lots of men's clothing stores on Maxwell Street. One day, my father decided he needed a new suit. So off we went to Maxwell Street to look for a suit at his favorite men's store. My dad found a suit he liked and was about to purchase it when he noticed it did not have a label. "What's this?" he said to the salesman. "This suit does not have a label."

The salesman said he would be right back and disappeared. A few minutes later, he returned with a small box filled with labels. "What label would you like?" he said to my dad. "Kupenheimer, Hart, Schaffner and

Marx..." He rattled off several more brand names. My dad picked out a label, the label was sewn into the suit coat, and off we went.

Most of these stores had a hawker standing out front. It was the hawker's job to entice you to come into the store by informing you that they had the best merchandise at the lowest prices. As you walked by, they would shout out, "Hey, boychik, come on in. We got the best deals." These hawkers were so good they could tell what part of Chicago you lived in. During my teenage years, after the Zucker family had moved to the affluent suburb of Lincolnwood, I made a trip to Maxwell Street. The hawker looked at how I was dressed and said, "Hey, Lincolnwood, Skokie." You had to be careful what you bought on Maxwell Street, though. The goods were not always exactly as advertised. I remember hearing one story of some boys who purchased men's dress shirts at a rock-bottom price. When they opened the shirts later at home, they discovered the shirts were for undertakers to use at wakes: they had no backs! Buyer beware. Of course, Roosevelt Road and Maxwell Street are long gone today as centers of Jewish entrepreneurial activity.

**Lunch in the Walnut Room at Marshall Field's, Christmas 1959
(With permission of the Chicago History Museum)**

But Roosevelt Road and Maxwell Street were not the only places the Zucker family shopped. We also made trips to downtown Chicago (a.k.a. the Loop) to shop at legendary upscale department stores such as Marshall Field's. This giant department store was built in the early twentieth century and remains a landmark in Chicago. Today, it is still in business but is now owned and operated by Macy's.

I made visits to Field's and other downtown department stores, most often with my mother. These were outings that I remember today with great fondness. My mother never learned to drive, so we took the electric train from the 87th Street station, which was only about a fifteen-minute walk from our house to the Loop. There were little shops at the station. While we were waiting for the train, my mother would buy me an Orange Crush drink and perhaps a six-pack of the little wax bottles filled with a sweet liquid that were popular then. When we arrived, it was only a short walk to Field's.

It's hard to describe today how glorious Field's was in the 1950s. It had everything: fine jewelry; beautiful clothing for men, women, boys, and girls; home furnishings; and a wonderful toy section. A trip to Field's was quite the opposite of one to Roosevelt Road. Women loved to wear hats in the 1950s, so my mom would always spend time in the millinery section of the store before we headed to the toy department. Some of the clothing I wore as a child also came from Field's, especially the striped T-shirts that were so in vogue then. Many of the Christmas gifts I purchased for my mom came from Field's. She loved the little porcelain bird statues the store sold.

Soon we would grow hungry, and it would be time to visit the beautiful Walnut Room on the seventh floor for lunch. The Christmas season was a wonderful time to go because a giant, beautifully decorated Christmas tree occupied the center of the tearoom. I believe I ordered the same item every time I lunched there: a delicious hamburger that came with a wonderful chili sauce. My wife, of course, made trips downtown with her mother as a child growing up in Lincolnwood. Only she ordered the "hen in the basket" instead of the hamburger for lunch. She was likely to come home with a new doll. And no visit to Field's was complete without taking home a box of scrumptious Frango mints.

Field's, though, was not the only store we visited downtown. There was Carson Pirie Scott & Co. We also visited Vaughn's. This was a smaller quirky store that had a lot of interesting things to look at. For example, it had an extensive collection of the miniature lead soldiers my brother and I loved to collect. There was also a talking parrot in a cage to greet you as you entered the store. On the way in, the bird said, "Goodbye"; on the way out, it said "Hello." Around three or four in the afternoon, we would walk back to the train station for the journey back to 8610 Rhodes Avenue. My wife and I have visited the Loop many times as adults, and it is just not the same. It has—like so many things in America today—lost its charm.

The 1950s and 1960s were preeminently the age of the automobile in the United States. In the early 1950s, dealers were selling over five million units annually; by the late 1960s, the number had swelled to almost ten million. As the middle class grew, following the expansion of American industry, more and more families were in a position to purchase a new car. In fact, it was common to trade in the old jalopy for a brand-new vehicle every two or three years.

Nowadays, most vehicles do not change from one year to the next. A major redo resulting in an all-new vehicle may take place every five years or so. Back then, the styling of cars could change dramatically from one year to the next. As the time came for the unveiling of the new Chevrolet, for example, the excitement would grow palpable throughout our neighborhood. Of course, in the 1950s, there were more places to drive than in previous decades, owing to the expansion of the highway system since the pre–World War II era. Who from my generation can forget the *The Dinah Shore Chevy Show*? In fact, the very first car I remember my father driving was a Chevrolet. But that quickly got upgraded to a Pontiac and then a light-blue 1953 Oldsmobile 98. I have a wonderful painting in my study that my brother did when he was in seventh grade at Dixon Elementary School of the Zucker family driving through the bayous of Louisiana on our way to Miami during a spring break vacation. I would have been eight years old and my brother twelve.

A few memories of that vacation stand out in my mind: for example, the boat trip we took through the Everglades and the beautiful ocean and beach in Miami. A year or two later, we took another memorable family vacation over spring break to Los Angeles, stopping along the way in Palm Springs, where we had dinner in a fancy restaurant. We were

The Vanishing World Of My Chicago Childhood

thrilled when we spotted a famous movie star, Jeff Chandler, dining at a nearby table. Palm Springs was a small town then and gorgeous.

We also visited the Smoky Mountains on another vacation; we stayed in the then-beautiful resort town of Gatlinburg in a rustic cabin with a babbling brook behind it. How time can change things. About ten years ago, my wife and I drove from Austin to Belhaven, North Carolina, to visit her family. On the way, we drove through the area. Although Gatlinburg itself is still nice, the town next to Gatlinburg is an abomination of tourist traps and plastic galore. I could not wait to get out of there.

Of course, the family sedan also made shorter trips. Each summer (as I have already discussed), we loaded the car up and took off for northern Wisconsin. And then, of course, there was driving around Chicago itself. My father was something of a legendary driver in our neighborhood. He seemed to pay very little attention to what he was doing. This was before autos had AC, so in the summer, his window would be rolled down with his left arm hanging out. In his left hand, he would be clutching his Perfecto Garcia cigar. He would pull in his arm occasionally so he could puff on his smoke.

I remember one trip my brother and I made with my father driving. Our friends Tom and Dean were in the back seat. Somewhere along the way, my dad got in a lively discussion with the two boys (about what I don't remember). He spent as much time with his head turned toward them in the back seat conversing with them as he did looking forward. When the ride was over, the brothers laughed uproariously. They could not believe my father had not gotten into a wreck.

My father prided himself on being a middleman. He liked to help friends and relatives get good deals on everything from appliances to cars. By sending a friend or relative to an automobile dealership, he was assured of getting a good deal himself when it came time to swap the family sedan for a new one. In 1957, he decided it was time to buy a new car. So the 1953 Oldsmobile was replaced by a gorgeous 1957

Oldsmobile 98. This one had a pink exterior ("desert glow" was the official color) with a gray vinyl interior.

In the 1950s, it was common to order your new vehicle from the dealer with exactly the amenities you wanted. When the order was placed, it would be sent to the General Motors factory, where the vehicle would be built to your exact specifications. This usually took three to four weeks. The big day would arrive when the dealer notified my dad the new Oldsmobile was in. We couldn't wait to drive to the dealer to pick it up.

This was an era when many iconic cars were produced, including, of course, the Ford Thunderbird and Chevy Corvette. The mid-1950s produced automobiles whose styling was meant to convey a sense of being modern. This resulted in vehicles that, well, looked sort of like airplanes. The epitome of this styling may well have been the 1957 Chrysler 300 C. My personal favorite from that era was the Studebaker Golden Hawk. Convertibles were also much more popular than they are now, no doubt because AC had not yet become common. An online article in *Motor Trend* (June 24, 2010) states that the 1940 Packard was the first car to offer factory-installed AC; by 1969, more than half of all new cars sold were equipped with AC. One big difference between then and now, though, is that, to the best of my recollection, almost all the families in our neighborhood owned only one car. That did change for the Zucker family during our last year on the South Side of Chicago. My father bought a used 1955 red-and-white Chevrolet for my brother to drive. By that time, Joe was a senior at Hirsch High School.

Discovering Girls and a Changing Culture

The few women who read earlier drafts of this work commented that the text hardly ever mentioned girls. There's a reason for that. From the time the Zucker family moved into the house at 8610 Rhodes Avenue when I was a small child until I entered the seventh grade, girls had very little to do with my life. My boyhood pals and I pretty much ignored them—until we started to enter puberty. Then the situation abruptly changed.

The problem we all faced, of course, was that the 1950s were incredibly repressive when it came to matters of sex. I remember my mother whispering to her friend Deborah E. that one of the younger women in the neighborhood had become pregnant. It seemed like a mystery to me how this had happened, and I could not understand why they were so secretive about it. We knew nothing. This made coping with the changes we were experiencing in our bodies and in our minds even more difficult.

Sinai Temple, beacon of progressivism that it was, decided it would offer a sex education class for its confirmation students. In this regard, Sinai was ahead of its time. The classes, of course, were separate for boys and girls. I remember my father and mother driving me to Sinai for the instruction. The educator spent an hour or so talking about sex. He did not have any actual visual aids but instead used a blackboard to draw some primitive illustrations. I remember leaving the class even more baffled than I was beforehand. My parents, nervous about the whole affair, made matters worse by joking on the way home that I was "now a man." To say I felt embarrassed would be an understatement.

The lack of any decent sex education naturally did not deter me from having crushes. I, along with just about every boy in the eighth grade, was smitten with Mary, a pretty girl sporting the ponytail hairstyle so popular in the 1950s. Eventually, I would begin to attend social affairs. So many teenagers back then got their first kiss playing spin the bottle. However, I seem to have missed out on that experience. I did begin to attend "formal" dances that were organized for the adolescents by the parents. These were awkward affairs with the boys on one side of the dance floor and the girls on the other.

In the eighth grade, Joan was my first serious crush. I remember walking home with her holding hands. One of my first actual dates was with Gerie, whom I invited to a splash party. Since I was not yet of driving age, my father drove us to the event. I sat in the front seat while my date sat in the back seat. Oy vey. (As I got older, my dating expertise fortunately would improve.) Based on the reading I have done about becoming an adolescent male in the 1950s, my experience was not atypical. I do not imagine the situation was much better for girls growing up in the 1950s.

TV began to have a major impact on teenage culture. The *American Bandstand* show, hosted by Dick Clark beginning in 1956, was wildly popular. The local version of his show was *Chicago Bandstand*, hosted by David J. Hull from the Merchandise Mart downtown. As an eighth grader, I remember attending this televised sock hop with a bunch of Dixon students. For some reason, we thought we were the only students invited that day, but when we arrived, we discovered students from dozens of schools. Still, it was exciting to be on TV.

The TV bandstand phenomenon reached millions of viewers by the late 1950s before it began to taper off. What music would we have been dancing to? Rock and roll, of course. The era in which I became a young teenager was one of monumental change in American popular music. Much of this change was generated by the influence of "race music" on white culture: black musicians not only were performing at the bandstand shows in person, but they were also influencing young white musicians. So we would have been dancing to black performers such as Chubby Checker, Little Richard, Fats Domino, and Sam Cooke and white performers such as Bill Haley and the Comets, Danny and the Juniors, and Jerry Lee Lewis. The sock hops, though, did not have mixed-race audiences until much later—a sad reflection on the state of American culture in the 1950s.

Perhaps the greatest rock and roll star of the era, though, was the immortal Elvis Presley, whose first big hit song, "Don't Be Cruel," hit the top of the charts in the summer of 1956. Parents were shocked by his gyrations—a portent of things to come. Fortunately, on the way out was a culture based on songs like Patti Page performing "How Much Is That Doggie in the Window?"

One would think a TV show called *The Mickey Mouse Club* wouldn't have held much interest for preteen and teenage boys, but it did. According to Wikipedia, the original show ran from 1956 to 1959. The host was Jimmie Dodd, a songwriter who provided leadership on and off the screen. The main cast members were called Mouseketeers and performed a variety of musical and dance numbers. Undoubtedly the roll call at the opening of the show was the most popular segment for teenage boys—me included. This was when each of the Mouseketeers would appear in front of their camera and shout out their names. The half dozen or so preteen and teenage girls who answered the roll call were all attractive, but one stood out among all the rest: the beautiful Annette Funicello, adorned in her slightly fuzzy Mouseketeer sweater. Funicello would go on from *The Mickey Mouse Club* to have a successful career as a singer and actress.

CHAPTER VII

Adult Social Activities and Relationships in Business and the Professions

My Parents' Social Activities

Although this story is about my childhood memories growing up on the South Side of Chicago, I would be remiss if I did not include memories of what my parents' lives were like. In fact, I believe their social activities were as different from those of today's parents, if not more so, as childhood activities then and now. What strikes me is how social adults were back then. At the beginning of this memoir, I remarked about how connected the people who lived around us were. In fact, it was a neighborhood. I have watched that change in contemporary America as more and more people move from the cities to the suburbs.

As I mentioned earlier, my parents belonged to a gin rummy club—a dozen or more friends getting together to play cards once a month at someone's house, followed by a big spread of food and drinks. I still remember those parties. And again, my parents became close friends with our builder and his family. Since we knew most of the families in our immediate neighborhood, informal visiting back and forth was common. My father had a whole slew of friends—quite a few of them people he had met while betting on the ponies at Arlington Park. Several of his customers also became close friends.

Irv and Leah also often went out on the town, but I do not have any specific recollections of where they went. Perhaps to see a movie or have dinner with friends. This was an era when people got dressed up, so my dad would have been wearing a suit or sports coat and my mom a fancy dress and a hat she had probably purchased at Marshall Field's or Carson Pirie Scott & Co. At some point, as the Zucker family became more affluent, my dad bought Leah a mink stole. Mink stoles and full-length mink coats were a sign you had "made it." Conspicuous consumption was the order of the day. During the cultural revolution of the late 1960s and 1970s, young people (including me) rejected these values. We chose to identify with the proletariat by wearing blue jeans and work shirts.

Interestingly, my wife has similar recollections of her parents' social activities while she was growing up in the suburb of Lincolnwood, where we would later meet. Shaya's dad, Herbert Gornstein, was a doctor who practiced on the North Side of the city and in the suburbs. My mother-in-law, Ginger, loved to make friends and to entertain. She had big dinner parties with perhaps as many as a dozen guests. Shaya's family was so close to some of the neighbors on Morris Avenue that they became honorary aunts and uncles. Herbert and Ginger also belonged to a community theater group.

Like me, Shaya had a huge number of relatives living in the countryside—her mother's clan hailed from the area around Belhaven, North Carolina. Each summer, the Gornsteins would first visit Herbert's relatives in New York and then head down the coast to visit Ginger's relatives. After Shaya and I were married, I wound up teaching at Fayetteville State University in North Carolina. Every two or three weeks, Shaya and I would make the three-hour drive to visit her relatives, who quickly adopted me as one of their own.

My mother had her own social network. Since very few if any of the women in our neighborhood worked outside the home, they had plenty of time to visit. She was particularly close to Deborah E, Calvin and Jeff's mom who lived on the next street over on Vernon Avenue. My memory is that pretty much on a weekly basis, they would get together for tea or coffee. This almost seemed like a ritual to me. Of course, I do not know what they talked about, but I do remember they always praised how nice each other's house looked. I think this was particularly important to people like my mother, whose life had not been easy growing up in semi-poverty after my grandfather became disabled in the train wreck.

Then, of course, there were my mother's nursing friends from her days at Ravenswood Hospital. I am not sure exactly when she retired—almost certainly after my parents got married. One of my mother's friends, Mack, I still remember, though not very well. My mother's nursing friends were frequent visitors at our home for dinner. Unfortunately, they had a habit of talking shop during dinner and frequently went into the details of gory operations. My brother often remarked to me how traumatized he was by these stories.

It is my contention that the number and frequency of contact among both children and adults in American society has declined since my childhood. If I am correct, what could be some of the reasons for the change? I think there are several.

First, I do not believe that middle-class people worked as hard or as many hours as they do today. My father was a good example of this. With a two-year diploma from Tuley High School in Chicago, he became a successful salesman for Federated Metals. Because of the numerous favors he had done for his customers during WWII, they were loyal to him. So I don't remember him scrambling for new customers while trying desperately to hold on to the old ones. Much of the time he spent with customers involved two-martini lunches. As I discussed previously, during the summers, he was often at the racetrack betting on the ponies when he theoretically should have been working. I remember my mother being happy Irv was out of the house. Of course, I cannot comment with any degree of accuracy on how many hours dads in our neighborhood worked. But I suspect, on average, it was significantly fewer than today.

It is important to remember that the United States emerged from WWII as the preeminent and unchallenged power in the world. The economy was booming. Unions were strong, negotiating well-paying jobs with eight-hour days, great retirement benefits, and vacation time. Layoffs were rare. Job security was high. You could have a working-class job and live a middle-class lifestyle. Many blue-collar working-class and white-collar middle-class employees who were hired by an American corporation while in their twenties or thirties could expect to retire from that same company. My dad was one of them. The dog-eat-dog world that was to emerge later for American workers was still far down the road.

Few if any women in my neighborhood worked at all. This meant, in the Chatham-Avalon of the 1950s, they had time to socialize and to participate in the PTA and other volunteer activities. I know this sounds socially conservative, but I believe women were the glue that largely held communities like Chatham-Avalon together. My mother retired from nursing to raise her two boys. (I know, that was enough of a job in and of itself.) She was an extremely bright woman, and I often wonder if she ever became bored with her stay-at-home life. Unfortunately, I never got to ask because, as I have mentioned, she passed away when I was in college. My sense is there was a trade-off for my mother. She had had to work hard as a young woman, helping support her invalid parents back in Antigo, and was happy overall to enjoy her beautiful home, her flowers, and I would like to think raising her children on Rhodes Avenue. Today, it often takes two incomes to support a middle-class lifestyle. Middle-class married women are now an integral part of the workforce. They often work as many if not more hours than their husbands at demanding jobs. This leaves them less time to socialize with neighbors, to become active in community activities, or to plan dinner parties.

A good example of these changes is illustrated by my work experience with the Texas State Teachers Association. In 1988, my wife, two sons, and I moved to Austin, where I became the executive director of the brand-new Texas Faculty Association. TFA was the higher education division of the Texas State Teachers Association, a very large organization founded in 1880. For many decades, TSTA did not have much competition for members. If you were a teacher, you joined TSTA. But that changed in the 1970s.

In 1974, the more than 100,000 members of TSTA voted by a substantial majority to affiliate with the National Education Association (NEA)—an organization that was, by that time, committed to unions and collective bargaining. As a result of the merger, TSTA dues skyrocketed. Many of the more politically conservative members of TSTA quit in droves after the merger to join a more traditional teachers association. In the following decades, TSTA was also challenged on the left by the more militant Texas Federation of Teachers, an affiliate of the American Federation of Teachers.

What this meant was that, when I joined the TSTA staff in 1988, the organization was hemorrhaging members. So what had once been a rather laid-back professional organization that could pretty much count on teachers to join when they graduated from college now had to scramble to recruit new members to its ranks. Positions had to be cut because TSTA was running up horrendous budget deficits. This did not make for a happy situation for the remaining staff, who were expected to do their old jobs plus pick up some of the responsibilities of their departed colleagues.

I was in pretty much the same boat. TFA was being heavily subsided by NEA; our membership had to grow each quarter, or it would be curtains for us. It was an incredibly stressful time to be a TSTA employee. In fact, the stress greatly affected my mental well-being.

One day while I was rummaging around in a closet at TSTA looking for office supplies, much to my surprise, I came upon a bunch of old photographs of a TSTA baseball team with some trophies the team had won. I thought to myself, *What the heck is this stuff?* After talking to some of the TSTA old-timers, I learned that decades before, TSTA indeed had had a baseball team that played in a league. If memory serves, the team comprised both men and women. They were apparently quite good. I was flabbergasted. *How in hell did they find the time to play in a baseball league?* I thought to myself.

Not content to let the matter rest, I began thinking about forming a team of some kind to represent TSTA. After doing a little research, I discovered a bowling league composed of teams representing professional associations headquartered in Austin. So I put out the call, got some recruits, and formed a TSTA bowling team. We had a five-member team (plus a few alternates, including my wife) and competed one night a week at a local bowling alley. The experiment was a great success. The morning after we competed, I would send out a brief "news release" to our Austin staff, recounting the glorious victories and, yes, the ignominious defeats from the night before. I am convinced the TSTA bowling team helped improve morale, and it was great fun for the team members. But it was tough to keep the team going in light of our hectic schedules.

Although my work experience at TSTA might seem unique, it was symbolic of a change that was taking place all over the United States. Beginning in the late 1970s, the manufacturing sector of the American economy went into a tailspin from which it has never recovered. Competition with manufacturers in foreign countries, which paid their employees a fraction of what American workers made, caused corporations to move their plants overseas and to cut salaries and benefits for the remaining workers at home. Manufacturing jobs were lost by the hundreds of thousands, especially in the Midwest. Labor unions, which were so strong in the 1950s and 1960s, went into a precipitous decline, hastened along by conservative anti-union politicians like

President Ronald Reagan. The idea that one paycheck could support a middle-class lifestyle went out the window for millions of families.

Second, the women's liberation movement took millions of women out of the home beginning in the 1970s. Let me make clear at the outset that I am a big fan of women's liberation (though my wife might disagree with that). I am old enough that my college years at the University of Wisconsin (1962–1966) preceded women's liberation. Most of the women I knew at Wisconsin majored in subjects like French and English literature. For many, the number one goal was to find a husband during their four years at college. The overwhelming majority of women who majored in a professional field went into education, library science, and so forth—thinking they would work as teachers, librarians, et cetera until they found a husband. Barbara, my girlfriend during my freshmen year at Wisconsin, was an exception. Her parents were both attorneys, and after graduating college, she went on to law school.

Women began demanding equality in the workplace in terms of both opportunities and salaries. And they began to move into professions such as medicine, law, higher education, and engineering that had been largely closed to them before. This certainly was a long overdue and wonderful development. But I believe it had its downside: women no longer stayed at home. The advent of both adults working full-time jobs meant that life became more hectic. There was less time to spend with the kiddies and socializing with other adults. Volunteering—always a mainstay of middle-class women—began to decline precipitously. Am I suggesting women should quit their jobs and go back to being stay-at-home moms? No. But I am suggesting that the massive entry of middle-class women into the workforce, either out of necessity or because of a desire to have a fulfilling career, had a negative impact on children and adults alike within the family. And, of course, as the American economy began to tank in the 1970s, two incomes became a necessity for millions of American families.

Third, TV and more recent electronic forms of electronic entertainment—most notably the smartphone, the internet, and digital computer games—have had an enormous impact on socializing. In my youth and even into my early adulthood, when you went to visit someone, you actually visited. People sat down in the living room and conversed with one another. This often included the children, though it was common for my brother and me disappear in order to play with the kids we were visiting: for example, our first cousins, Ken Jr. and Connie Pride. But we were actually playing—not watching TV or hooked into an electronic game. Some of the articles I have read about the entertainment habits of teenagers today indicate they spend as many as nine hours per day plugged into electronic games or social media.

Relationships in Business and the Professions

I believe the decline in social relationships among both children and adults in contemporary America goes part and parcel with a decline in personal relations in business and the professions. The Chicago—indeed, the America—in which I grew up had far fewer nationwide corporations than the America of the twenty-first century. Yes, we had General Motors, General Electric, and hundreds of other corporations, but they were not nearly as pervasive and omnipresent as they are today. Fast food chains were just in their infancy. The first McDonald's in Chicagoland was opened in Des Plaines in 1955. Although shopping malls date from the 1920s, there were very few of them in Chicagoland when I was growing up. Old Orchard, the giant shopping mall located in Skokie, did not open until 1956. So individual businesspeople owned most stores, shops, and so forth. As a result, there was a kind of connection between the customer and the business owner that has largely disappeared from American society.

Take barbershops, for example. My dad would always take my brother and me to get our hair cut at the same barbershop, located a few miles from our home. Okay, the haircuts were generally lousy. But the barber knew who we were by name. Today, when I go to get my hair cut in San Antonio, it's in a business owned and operated by a giant nationwide chain, such as Supercuts. This hair salon franchise has more than 2,400 locations across the United States. I can expect my hairstylist to introduce himself or herself ("Hi, my name is Ron" or "Hi, my name is Cindy.") and to ask me what kind of haircut I would like, and twenty minutes later, I am out the door. I may never see my hairstylist again, or, if I do, they have forgotten who I am, and vice versa. The same thing is true of drugstores, sporting goods stores, grocery stores, et cetera. As I mentioned at the start of this tome, my parents knew the builder of our house at 8610 Rhodes Avenue personally, and we became good friends with his family. Try that when you are purchasing a house in a new subdivision of several hundred homes.

The nature of relationships between practitioners of the medical arts and their patients has also changed. In my family, doctors were revered. Of course, the fact that my mother was a registered nurse who had worked closely with many wonderful doctors at Ravenswood Hospital before she retired to raise her children certainly had something to do with this. But I believe what was true for my family was true for many if not most families in our neighborhood. What has changed? For one thing, doctors actually made house calls. Can you believe that? As a child, I remember our family doctor making a house call when one of us was sick. It was comforting to have the doctor standing by your bedside. Of course, the Zucker family also made visits to our doctors as well. In short, the doctor knew you and your family. In fact, my father-in-law, Dr. Herbert Gornstein, made house calls routinely as a young physician, growing his practice on the North Side of Chicago. In several instances, he delivered a baby for a mother and then, years later, a baby for her daughter. Patients stopped by his office to deliver presents at Christmastime. Admittedly, in light of the traffic jams that plague major American cities today, it would seem inefficient to have doctors traveling from house to house to see patients.

Most of us in recent decades have had pretty much the same experience visiting the doctor. Your appointment is for ten a.m., but you are not called in to see the doctor until ten forty-five a.m. But, of course, even then you don't see the doctor right away. Instead, you are ushered into an examining room where a nurse takes your vital signs, and you read old magazines until the doctor arrives around eleven fifteen a.m. If you are lucky, you are out the door by eleven forty-five a.m. And this timeline does not even take into account the hour or so you spend traveling back and forth from the doctor's office.

With the rise of urgent care centers in the last few decades, visiting the doctor is pretty much like getting your hair trimmed at Supercuts. You see the nurse practitioner, physician's assistant, or maybe, if you are lucky, an actual doctor. But it is usually a one-time shot—unless you have to return for additional care. Does this loss of a personal connection between a medical practitioner and a patient actually make a difference in the quality of care you receive? I believe it does, although I do not have any scientific studies to back up that assertion. What I strongly believe is that having a doctor who knows their patients has a positive psychological effect on them—at least, it does for me.

Another practitioner of the healing arts whom the Zuckers frequented was our dentist, Dr. John J. Dr. J. built his office building on 83rd Street—right across from Dixon Elementary School. I believe I had my first visit to see him when I was perhaps seven or eight. As a child, I began developing cavities that would plague me throughout my life. Chicago began putting fluoride in its water in 1956, but apparently that was too late to be of any help to me. In the 1950s, the dental arts had not made the connection between guzzling massive amounts of Coca-Cola, chomping on endless amounts of candy, and tooth decay. The Zucker boys were not the only kids in the neighborhood who consumed too much sugar from soft drinks. The joke was that one of our neighborhood pals drank so much root beer his parents had a tap installed with root beer flowing out of it instead of water.

Dr. J. operated his dental business by himself. He did not have either a receptionist or a dental hygienist. My mother would make an appointment for me to see him after school let out. I would walk the short distance to his office where he would be waiting for me. Often, my appointments took much longer than needed because Dr. J. liked to talk and he found both my brother and me to be interesting patients. What did we talk about? I remember that we talked a lot about cars. His hobby was restoring antique automobiles, and the storage room in his office was loaded with car parts that he had ordered. One conversation that has stuck with me over the years had to do with the Cadillac Motor Car Company. One advertisement for Cadillac sometime in the 1950s bragged that the company's brand-new vehicle was so quiet the only thing you could hear from the inside was the clock ticking. I remember him chuckling as he said to me, "Why would you build an expensive car like that where you could hear the clock ticking? The clock should be quiet."

He was also an amateur violinist and would frequently take his instrument out of its case and play a tune for me. One of the more unusual things about Dr. J's dentistry was that he did not believe in using anesthesia when filling cavities. Why that was I don't know. Okay, I never claimed he was a particularly good dentist. (Oh, by the way, the candy store was right next to his office. So before walking home, I would stop in, plop down a dime or fifteen cents, and buy myself some treats, thus ensuring more visits to the dentist.)

Today, in San Antonio, I have a wonderful dentist. He, too, is the only dentist in his practice. But unlike Dr. J., he has two receptionists and a whole coterie of dental assistants. The people who work for him are remarkably friendly, though. And I have had some terrific conversations, in particular with one of his assistants who grew up in South Texas. We have compared notes about our childhoods while I was waiting for the anesthesia to kick in. What I discovered was that her childhood as a Hispanic American growing up on the border was strikingly similar to mine on the South Side of Chicago.

Of course, the personal touch in relations between a business owner or a professional and a customer has not disappeared entirely. I am convinced, again without any supporting statistical evidence, that such relationships are much more likely to exist today in small towns. For over a decade, my wife and I have been fortunate to own a summer home outside Columbia Falls, Montana. "C Falls," as locals call it, has a population of maybe four thousand souls. The town has several barbershops, but my favorite is the Barber's Chair, located on the main drag. Barbara, the proprietor, has been cutting my hair for many years. There's always two or three customers waiting to get their hair trimmed and an interesting discussion on some subject or another underway: for example, the fire burning in a nearby national forest, the endless delays caused by road construction in Montana during the summer, or the flood of tourists who have descended on the town. Sadly, Barbara has recently sold her shop to a new owner.

Next door to the Barber's Chair is Bad Rock Books, a used bookstore owned by Cindy that also sells some new books. I have known Cindy for years and always stop in her store several times during the summer. She now carries my book, *A Fisherman's Journey*, a memoir of my fishing experiences with my family and friends covering seventy years. I am frequently amazed when I am shopping at Smith's grocery store by the interaction among the customers and between the customers and the employees. They all seem to know each other. That simply does not happen when I am shopping at the mega grocery stores in San Antonio.

People still seem to have the time to converse with one another in northwest Montana. Several years ago, a friend came to visit us to do some fly-fishing. I informed Mike on the phone before he departed that it was customary when you met a person in our neck of the woods to begin the conversation by asking them how the fishing has been, and vice-versa. Sure enough, after he arrived, almost everybody we met started the conversation by talking about fly-fishing: Where were we trying our luck, what flies were we using, and—most importantly— were we catching any?

Years ago, before our beloved Old English sheepdog, Sarie, passed away, I would take her to our local veterinarian, Mark. Mark is an intrepid fly-fisherman who moved from a high-powered practice in Atlanta to Columbia Falls to enjoy life more. Before he even looked at Sarie, we typically would spend fifteen minutes or so discussing fly-fishing. And finally, there was the legendary Stumptown Angler, a fly-fishing shop in Whitefish owned by David. I would stop by his shop to buy a few flies or leaders and emerge an hour later. There were always people in his store talking, of course, about fly-fishing. Try that when you are ordering your fly-fishing supplies from AvidMax.

Why, you may ask, do I raise this issue in a memoir about my childhood? It is because I believe the same social forces that affect the lives children lead today have also changed the lives of adults. Personal relationships are not what they were when I was a kid. The number and frequency of close relationships in all walks of life are on the decline in modern America. And, sadly, since the population in northwest Montana is now exploding, I am starting to see some unfortunate changes taking place there.

CHAPTER VIII

The Great Migration, a Changing Neighborhood, and the Flight to the Suburbs

This chapter is painful for me to write because it raises the sensitive issue of race relations in the Chatham-Avalon community in which I grew up. Owing to social and economic forces beyond the Zucker family's control, our neighborhood would change from one that was entirely non-Hispanic Caucasian to one that was overwhelmingly African American within the space of three or four years. The reasons for the great migration of African Americans from the Southern states to the North have been well documented. Facing oppressive segregation laws, lynchings, and abject poverty following World War I, African Americans began moving in huge numbers to many major northern cities, including New York, Detroit, and, of course, Chicago. Although conditions were far from ideal for African Americans in post–World War I northern cities, they were far better than in the South. Yes, discrimination was rampant in housing, employment, and schooling, but the degree of freedom African Americans enjoyed in cities like Chicago far surpassed anything they had experienced in Alabama, Mississippi, Georgia, or South Carolina. No wonder African Americans began pouring into Chicago after WWI. In 1920, Chicago's Black population was about 78,000; by 1950, it had increased to approximately 356,000. With such an exploding population, Black families needed places to live. Inevitably, they began to move into neighborhoods that were inhabited by white people. Chatham-Avalon was one of them.

Racism was a powerful force among the white population of the Chatham-Avalon in which I was raised. Many of our neighbors believed Black people were inherently inferior. Some of my neighborhood pals and their parents engaged in demeaning African-Americans. Others were more circumspect in what they thought of Black people. I do not remember anyone in our neighborhood discussing the possibility that somehow Chatham-Avalon could be successfully integrated. I have read there were community organizations that tried to bring about the integration, but I did not hear about them at the time our neighborhood was changing. I am not certain when the first discussions began among our neighbors about the fact that African Americans were moving into Chatham-Avalon, but I believe it must have been in the late 1950s. The fear was that if you waited too long to put your house on the market, you would take a big hit because it was believed, at some point, property values would decline. So you did not want to be the first to put a For Sale sign in the front yard, but you did not want to be among the last, either. I believe we were somewhere in the middle.

As Jews who attended the ultra-progressive Sinai Temple, I believe our family was more conflicted about the situation than many of our neighbors. My mother, who had converted to Reform Judaism, had shared the values of Sinai long before she met my dad. Her favorite political figure was Eleanor Roosevelt. In spite of what had happened during the Holocaust, though, Jews, too, could be guilty of prejudice. I can't remember my father ever launching into an anti-Black tirade, but he shared the racial prejudice that was common among many Jews in the 1950s (and, I am afraid, for many more decades and even today).

Complicating the relationship between Jews and African Americans in Chicago was the fact that many Jewish shop owners served a primarily Black clientele. Consequently, friction often erupted between the two groups. It was not uncommon for Blacks to accuse Jewish shop owners of ripping them off. In any case, I am sorry to say my father and many of our relatives often used derogatory terms when referring to African Americans. The most common one that I recall my Jewish relatives using was *schwarzer*, which means Black person in Yiddish. I can't say for certain the N-word was never used in my house, but if so, it was rare. If all this sounds like an apology, it is. But like millions of white Americans back then (and I am afraid even now) I was raised in a climate where both ethnic and racial prejudices were omnipresent.

I do not remember in what grade the first African American students showed up in my classroom at Dixon. I do know that by the time I had reached the eighth grade, the number of white and Black students in my class was pretty evenly divided. I have documentation for this because I still have a photograph of the group. To say the arrival of Black students in ever-increasing numbers caused consternation among both white parents and the school administration would be an understatement. It was something akin to full-fledged panic. The white community simply could not accept the fact that Dixon had become a multiracial institution.

In fact, during the fall semester of my eighth-grade year, something happened that seems astonishing today. My mother received a phone call from the principal's office stating that he wanted to see both her and me. We had no idea what it was about. On the day of the appointment, we were ushered into his office on the first floor. After a few pleasantries, the principal came to the point. He said that since the Negro students (I can't be sure he used the term *Negro*) were "ruining the school" and since I was considered an exceptionally bright student, there wasn't any point in me sticking around for the second semester of eighth grade. So, with my parents' permission, he wished to use his authority as principal to have me "skip" the spring semester at Dixon; I would graduate at the end of the fall term. There must have been a family discussion of his offer that evening. In the end, my parents decided to accept it. I would begin attending Hirsch High School in January 1959.

This decision was to have a profound impact on my life—more than either my parents or I could have imagined at the time. But that part of my autobiography goes well beyond the years covered here. In retrospect, his decision, based on the changing demographics of Dixon, did not make any sense. Hirsch High School's proportion of Black to white students, if anything, was greater than Dixon's. So why did he do it? I really don't have a clue. Perhaps he felt like the captain of a ship about to be overrun by pirates.

My eighth-grade graduation photo at Dixon Elementary School
(Source: Zucker family photo)

What is Dixon Elementary School like today? It has an impressive website that both my brother and I have visited on several occasions. Photos of the school show it is attractive and well maintained. The website states that the school is located "in the Chatham neighborhood, which has been a predominantly African American community since 1959," adding that many professional and business leaders have chosen the Chatham neighborhood for their home. Currently, Dixon has about 580 students, 99 percent of whom are African American. It is a "mathematics and science cluster school with an emphasis in fine arts, literacy, and technology."

Interestingly, before he passed away, my brother and I often discussed our desire to return to the old neighborhood to visit the school we attended as children. I still harbor the desire. In today's world, it isn't so easy for a stranger to visit a public school. Maybe I will write a letter to the principal or pick up the phone and call sometime down the road. But I had better not wait too long. I am running out of time.

At some point, the inevitable happened: A neighbor put up a For Sale sign. It did not take long for For Sale signs to begin popping up all over the neighborhood like mushrooms after a rainstorm. Soon, there was one in front of our house. I don't remember how long it took to sell, but I don't believe it was more than a few months. Interestingly, one of the prospective buyers for 8610 Rhodes Avenue was none other than Mr. Cub, Ernie Banks! Our realtor must have tipped my parents off that Ernie was coming to look at our house because we were on hand when he arrived for the showing. I remember being introduced to him and shaking hands out in front of our house.

To say there was some irony in this event would be an understatement. Banks was the first African American to play for the Cubs, breaking the color line on Thursday, September 17, 1953, when he was called up from the Kansas City Monarchs, one of the most successful teams in the Negro American League. The Cubs lost to the Philadelphia Phillies that day 16 to 4. An excellent article written by Steven Dunn for the Society for American Baseball Research describes the racial situation in Chicago that awaited Banks. Dunn cites famed Chicago columnist Mike Royko, who wrote that the only genuine difference between a Southern white and a Northern white was in their accent.[6] This may be somewhat of an exaggeration, of course. Although there certainly many nasty incidents involving race hatred and violence perpetrated against Black people in Chicago and the surrounding suburbs when I was growing up, it was not nearly as sever as what African-Americans experienced in cities of the Deep South.

Mr. Cub was to become one of the most revered and loved Chicagoans of all time among whites and Blacks alike. During his career from 1953 to 1971, he thrilled Cubs fans with his signature line-drive home runs over the ivy-covered walls of Wrigley Field—512 in all. I witnessed quite a few of these in person and many more on TV. How is it that such a racist city came to idolize an African American baseball player? American race relations are filled with contradictions, and this is one of them. Part of Banks's appeal was his genuinely modest personality and his love of the game of baseball. Banks's famous saying, "Let's play two," endeared him to baseball fans. I have often thought that if Mr. Cub had been one of the relatively small number of African Americans to move into the Chatham neighborhood in the 1950s, the white residents' response to having Black neighbors might have been quite different. But that was not to be the case. I do not remember anything about the African American family who purchased our home. I doubt I ever met them.

What do I remember about the Black kids who began moving into our neighborhood? One memory stands out in particular. The E. Family moved out of their home on Vernon Avenue before we departed our home on Rhodes Avenue. Our new neighbors had a child my age. To this day, I remember meeting this boy out in the alley between our homes. What struck me about him was how nice he was. We talked to each other for perhaps five or ten minutes. Intuitively, I realized at

---

[6] Steve Dunn, "September 17, 1953: Ernie Banks Breaks the Color Line for the Cubs," Society for American Baseball Research, https://sabr.org/gamesproj/game/september-17-1953-ernie-banks-breaks-color-barrier-for-cubs/.

the time that something was wrong with what I had been told about Black people.

This brief encounter was to have a profound effect on my life—one I could not have realized at the time. I believe that, had the Zucker family stayed on Rhodes Avenue, this boy and I would have become friends. But we never had the chance. The situation at Dixon Elementary School between the Black students and the white students might best be described as strained, but I don't remember any overt racial conflict breaking out. I certainly talked to my new Black classmates, but I never made friends with any of them, either.

My mother, I believe, must have known for some time that the Zucker family would eventually be leaving our home at 8610 Rhodes Avenue. For several years, on our way up to northern Wisconsin, we stopped off to visit my father's cousins Reggie and Estelle Holzer, who lived in Lincolnwood—the first suburb north of Chicago. She had her eye on settling in this upscale community. So either shortly before or after we sold our house, my father purchased a lot at 6800 N. Kedvale Avenue. in Lincolnwood. Our new home would be a classic midcentury bi-level decked out with a spacious family room for the new color TV and stereo console. The only problem was that the house would not be completed until almost a year after we had to move out of 8610 Rhodes to make way for the new occupants.

My parents found a large apartment for us on Maryland Avenue—about three or four miles from the old homestead. It was comfortable enough, but that period of time was one of the most miserable in my family's life. We felt uprooted. The extra time on the South Side, though, allowed my brother to finish his senior year at Hirsch High School. I remember, on the day I graduated a semester early from Dixon, I rushed over to the gym to watch him score twenty-nine points against Hyde Park High School. So my brother and I spent one semester together at Hirsch High School—I as a freshman and he a senior. The following fall, Joe enrolled at Miami of Ohio University, while I started at Niles West Township High School.

CHARLES ZUCKER

Brother Joe and I standing in front of our 1957 Oldsmobile after we moved into the apartment on Maryland Avenue. (Source: Zucker family photo)

The culture of my new neighborhood was a radical departure from life on the South Side of Chicago. Instead of the sometimes rough-and-tumble environment in the Chatham community, similar to the one popularized (and sanitized) in the TV sitcom *Happy Days*, I found myself now in an upper-middle-class neighborhood. Since both Lincolnwood and neighboring Skokie had substantial Jewish populations, many of my new friends were Jews. That was also a big change from the Chatham neighborhood. This was definitely a community that was upward bound. My classmates wore Bermuda shorts and madras shirts and talked about what college they planned to attend and which fraternity they hoped to pledge in their freshmen year. Also, at first I thought I had fallen into a community populated by super athletes. As I made new friends, I discovered almost all of them had a space in their house devoted to their sports accomplishments: bookshelves were lined with trophies. Later on, I realized that, in the suburbs, the "culture of success" meant that kids received trophies for almost anything they did. They were not all super athletes after all.

Niles West did not have students entering in mid-semester, which meant I either had to go back one half year to the class I belonged in age-wise or go ahead another half year. After a battery of tests, the Niles West administration gave me the choice. After more discussions with my parents, I went ahead another half year. So I would graduate from high school one year early and head off to the University of Wisconsin in Madison.

At Wisconsin, I eventually wound up majoring in history. This was a good major for me because my mathematical and science skills were mediocre at best. But I was good at reading and writing, and Wisconsin's history department was phenomenal. I took a number of courses in European history from the legendary history professor George Mosse, who was a Holocaust survivor. In my senior year, I was eligible to write an honors thesis. I chose as my subject African American congressmen during Reconstruction. Why this subject? In the old days, when students actually studied American history in grade school and high school, the textbook almost invariably included a photo of assembled "Negro congressmen" taken during the Reconstruction era. I often wondered who these serious-looking men were and what they were up to. I spent many hours in the library researching the subject and wrote a paper my honors director, Professor Sewall, considered first rate. (Okay, I am tooting my own horn here.)

In the fall of 1966, I entered Northwestern University's PhD program in history. As I progressed through graduate school, I became more and more interested in the history of American race relations. Fortunately, the same year I enrolled, NU hired George Fredrickson, who had just published his book *The Black Image in the White Mind*. Fredrickson would be my thesis adviser, and in 1972, I earned my PhD after completing my dissertation, "The Free Negro Question in Ante-Bellum

Illinois." This was, of course, the era when the civil rights movement was in full swing. Historians were discovering for the first time the extent and severity of racism in the northern states, including Illinois.

This was a subject I knew something about—firsthand. My first teaching job was at Fayetteville (North Carolina) State University, a historically Black university. I was on the faculty for two years before heading to Kent State University in Ohio where, for a year, I was a National Endowment for the Humanities postdoctoral fellow. My final teaching gig was at Carroll College in Waukesha, Wisconsin, where I taught a course entitled "Black and White in American History." While at Carroll, African American students were instrumental in starting an exchange program with Rust College, a Black institution of higher education in Holly Springs, Mississippi. I spent a January term as a visiting professor at Rust along with five students from Carroll. The Black students at Carroll presented me with a trophy for my role in helping to get the program going, which I still proudly display today.

Why do I bring all this up? Perhaps my motive is to demonstrate the extent to which I was able to overcome the racist climate that permeated the Chatham neighborhood in which I grew up. However, I believe there is another important point to be made here. Much has been written about the migration of African Americans to northern cities like Chicago and the effect it had on Black people. But almost nothing has been written about the myriad ways the migration affected the lives of whites in these neighborhoods. I believe the assumption is that prejudiced white people sold their homes to Black people and then fled to new digs far from the old neighborhood, where they continued their lives of prejudice. If history were only that simple.

Conclusion

The Zucker Family in Historical Perspective

Our Family as Transitional in the Midcentury United States

To say the Zuckers' experience on the South Side of Chicago during the 1950s took place at a time when European American families were in transition would be to say practically nothing. The fact is that from the time European Americans first got off the boat at Jamestown in 1607, European American families have been in a constant state of flux. So the real question is what the Zucker family was transitioning from and what it was transitioning to during the time we spent at 8610 Rhodes Avenue. And, more specifically, how was my childhood different from those who had gone before and those who were to come later? Several factors come to mind.

First, our family was a result of the ongoing assimilation that had started decades before and would continue to pick up steam in future decades. My mother's Protestant and Catholic ancestors hailed from the British Isles and Western Europe. My father's ancestors were Western

European Jews. Decades later, when my wife and I lived in Austin, Texas, we belonged to a synagogue whose adult members were more often than not from different religious backgrounds. My mother, as previously discussed, hailed from Antigo, Wisconsin—a small town in an overwhelmingly rural and agricultural area. She, like countless young men and women in the early decades of the twentieth century, decided to move to the city because of greater economic opportunities. Interestingly, my future mother-in-law followed much the same path, moving from rural eastern North Carolina to Washington, DC, to take up nursing—just as my mother had. Later, she would meet my father-in-law, a handsome young medical student whose Jewish ancestors came from Ukraine, then part of Russia.

Our family was also characterized by the upward mobility that followed the Great Depression and World War II. My father, with his two-year high school diploma, did extremely well financially. He was a good salesman and businessman. My father-in-law, whose family came from humble origins in Ukraine, became a highly successful doctor practicing on Chicago's North Side. The Zucker family was also affected by the great industrial and technological changes that had started in America in the nineteenth century and accelerated during the 1950s. Ours was the first generation to own a TV. We had a family sedan in which we could travel from one end of the country to the other on the brand-new interstate highway system. Because of my family's upward social and economic mobility, my brother and I were the first generation in our family to attend college. He flew off for his freshman year in an airplane from Midway Airport!

I believe the childhood and the world I experienced growing up on Chicago's South Side now is largely vanishing. Perhaps another way to describe it would be to say it is endangered.

I do not wish to reiterate everything I have written in the previous pages, but I believe the number and variety of childhood activities my brother and I and our neighborhood pals engaged in far surpassed what today's children experience. We played outside endlessly, and, when we were forced indoors because of the weather, the array of games we played again exceeded what I see going on with today's kids. Technologically, we were the first generation to spend hours in front of the TV, watching cartoons, westerns, variety shows, and more, yet it was a relatively small part of our experience. Today it seems kids are hooked into their electronics almost constantly when they are not in school. As mentioned earlier, one article I read stated that the average teenager spends nine hours per day on social media. In fact, I believe many parents have largely lost control of their children to the corporations that mesmerize their kids with endless electronic games.

Two Prophetic Works: The Movie *Avalon* and the Book *Bowling Alone*

My goal in writing this memoir is not to produce a piece of academic scholarship. However, I believe two brilliant works—one a movie and the other a book—together highlight the profound changes that have transformed American society and the American family over the last century. The first is the highly autobiographical 1990 movie *Avalon*, written and directed by Barry Levinson, and the second is the book *Bowling Alone: The Collapse and Revival of American Community* by Robert D. Putnam, published in 2000.

Avalon follows the lives of the five Krichinskys—Jewish brothers who all emigrated from Russia in the early twentieth century and settled in Baltimore. The main character in the movie, Sam Krichinsky, arrives in America on the Fourth of July and wonders at the beautiful fireworks he sees. The first-generation extended family—like millions of other European American immigrants—is close knit. The first Krichinskys to arrive pool their resources through hard work and are eventually able to bring over all the brothers and their families.

The extended family is the center of their social life. They live near one another, hold family councils, and pool their money for charitable giving and to help family members in need. Each subsequent generation drifts further away from the family circle. Two cousins of the second generation Americanize their names, open a huge appliance store, and become rich selling TVs. Eventually, one of the second-generation cousins moves to the suburbs.

A family rupture occurs when the other brother, who still lives in the city, has trouble finding the cousin's house and arrives late for Thanksgiving dinner. He is outraged when he discovers his brother has cut the turkey without him and leaves in a huff. The final time the brothers see each other is at a family council meeting where there's a huge blowup over the issue of providing financial support for Holocaust survivors who have immigrated to the United States. It's the last time the family council ever meets, and the brothers never speak again.

The huge extended family of the first generation has shrunk into nuclear families separated from one another. The suburban family is Mom, Dad, and two kids. When it's time for the Uncle Miltie show, they all rush into the living room to eat their dinners in front of the TV. Television is a disastrous invention that has cut human society off from its roots.

Perhaps the movie's view of immigrant life in America is romanticized. Yet, in the history of my own family, the movie seems remarkably prescient. Of all the uncles, aunts, and cousins in my father's and mother's families, I am barely in touch with anyone. On my father's side, my only remaining close contact was with my now-deceased brother. On my mother's side, I am friends with one cousin on Facebook.

TV and other forms of modern entertainment, though, are hardly solely to blame for this diminishment of my extended family. There's no doubt that geographical mobility and upward social mobility also played a big role in my family's loss of contact with relatives. It's true that if I were to reside in Wisconsin, I would be in touch with more relatives, many of whom live in towns like Oshkosh and Fond du Lac. But the gigantic clan of Prides and Rammers that was centered around Antigo when I was growing up has scattered like leaves in the wind. And if I were still living in the Chicago area, I can only think of one relative with whom I would be in touch.

Bowling Alone is a remarkable piece of scholarship that surveys the decline since 1950 in all forms of in-person social intercourse that Americans for countless generations used to found, educate, and enrich the fabric of their social lives. The author cites data from the General Social Survey to show there has been a steep decline since 1950 in the aggregate membership and number of volunteers participating in civic organizations such as the PTA, the Lions Club, the League of Women voters, the Red Cross, and dozens of others. In particular, he notes that church membership declined dramatically during the period from 1950 to 1990.

Putnam argues that this decline in what he refers to as "social capital" has produced serious social problems in American society as we become more and more isolated from each other. It even has profound implications, he argues, for the future of American democracy, arguing that people have become more distrustful of one another because of the growing isolation. Why is his book entitled *Bowling Alone*? One of the most intriguing facts he discovered was that, in 1990, Americans were bowling in larger numbers than ever. But guess what? They were no longer as likely to be bowling on a team in a league like the one I founded when employed by TSTA. Instead, they were more likely to be bowling in a small group—with a few friends, perhaps, or family members.

What factors does Putnam think are primarily responsible for this phenomenon? Not surprisingly, he views television as the main culprit. What started with my generation has turned into a form of entertainment that isolates us from contact with other human beings. But it's not just TV. In the 1960s, many members of my generation became obsessed with stereophonic equipment—including me. I remember spending hours poring over reviews of different speakers, receivers, turntables, and more. And finally the big day came when I purchased a new system. How exciting! Later, of course, I would need to add a CD player as LP records started to become obsolete.

Ironically, many of us who were involved in the cultural revolution of the 1960s and 1970s believed we were doing something different. We turned our backs (albeit temporarily) on our parents' love of watching TV. We deluded ourselves into thinking we were somehow revolutionary when the sad reality was we were just hooked on another technological entertainment innovation that also tended to separate us from contact with other human beings. In a wonderful talk at Harvard University (available on YouTube), Putnam describes how stereo equipment has affected his own life. He explains he used to enjoy attending concerts with a close friend. However, they had different tastes: Putnam enjoyed the classic composers, such as Beethoven and Mozart, while his friend liked twentieth-century composers, such as Hindemith. Eventually, they stopped going to concerts together and instead preferred to stay at home, where they could listen to the music each preferred on their high-fidelity systems. Compare this to what my wife remembers when, as a child, she visited her mother's family in rural eastern North Carolina. The extended family of aunts, uncles, and cousins got together to play their musical instruments—a good old-fashioned hootenanny.

Epilogue

The US Surgeon General's 2023 Advisory on the Healing Effects of Social Connection and Community

As I was finishing up a first draft of this work, Dr. Vivek H. Murthy, the nineteenth and twenty-first surgeon general of the United States, issued an advisory report on the epidemic of loneliness and isolation in American society. As Dr. Murthy began a cross-country listening tour in 2014 as the newly appointed surgeon general, he heard stories from his fellow Americans that surprised him. In his introduction to the advisory, Murthy writes that people told him they felt "isolated, invisible, and insignificant." He adds that even when people couldn't put their finger on the word *lonely*, that was what they meant. It was a "light bulb moment" for him as he came to realize that social disconnection was far more common than he had realized.

But the wealth of statistical information contained in the advisory demonstrates that loneliness is far more than just a bad feeling—it harms both individual and societal health. The surgeon general writes:

It is associated with a greater risk of cardiovascular disease, dementia, stroke, depression, anxiety, and premature death. The mortality impact of being socially disconnected is similar to that caused by smoking up to 15 cigarettes per day. And even greater than that associated with obesity and physical inactivity. And the harmful consequences of a society that lacks social connection can be felt in our schools, workplaces, and civic organizations, where performance, productivity, and engagement are diminished.[7]

In the section entitled "Current Trends: Is Social Connection Declining?" the surgeon general writes that across many measures, Americans appear to be becoming less socially connected over time. "Changes in key indicators" he writes, "including social participation, demographics, community involvement, and use of technology over time, suggest both overall societal declines in social connection and that, currently, a significant portion of Americans lack adequate social connection."[8]

The statistics Dr. Murthy uses to support his assertions dovetail with the argument I have made in this memoir regarding the decline of personal contact (and the quality of those interactions) among both children and adults in contemporary American society. Objective measures of "social exposure" obtained from 2003 through 2020 find "social isolation," measured by average time spent alone, increased dramatically in that time period, representing an average increase of twenty-four hours per month spent alone. At the same time, social participation across several types of relationships has steadily declined.

---

[7] Dr. Vivek H. Murthy, *Our Epidemic of Loneliness and Isolation: The U.S. Surgeon General's Advisory on the Healing Effects of Social Connection and Community,* 2023, p.4.

[8] Dr. Vivek H. Murthy, *Our Epidemic of Loneliness and Isolation: The U.S. Surgeon General's Advisory on the Healing Effects of Social Connection and Community,* 2023, pp. 13-15

The time spent with friends in person socially has decreased by twenty hours per month. The surgeon general notes that the decline is starkest for young people ages fifteen to twenty-four. For this age group, time spent with friends in person has been reduced by nearly 70 percent over almost two decades. Finally, there has been a sharp decline in close friendships over several decades. In the final chapter, he makes a bunch of recommendations regarding how to reverse the tide. I fear, however, that this advisory may soon be collecting dust on various library shelves as we continue to rush pell-mell into the future.

And so the Margaret Mead quote with which I began this work appears to have come to pass in my own lifetime. I was born into one kind of world, grew up in another, and am now living in yet quite a different world with my adult children and grandchildren. In fact, in the present moment (Spring 2025), the media is filled with raging debates about how artificial intelligence in the form of chatbots will cause life in the near future to be remarkably changed from what it is today—whether it will be for better or for worse, no one can be certain. However, in the midst of continuing change at a bewildering rate, one trend seems almost certain to continue: the decline of honest-to-goodness, face-to-face contact among human beings—unless, of course, as a society, we begin to take steps to reverse it.

Acknowldgements

During the pandemic, I began doing genealogical research on my family's ancestry. Through the wonders of Ancestry.com, I was unable to unearth an abundant amount of information about my both father's and my mother's descendants over the generations. I learned how they were related to one another, where they lived, how many children they had, what they did for a living, when they were born, when they passed away and so forth. It was exciting at first, but then I found myself growing frustrated because I realized that I knew little or nothing about their personal lives. So, I decided to focus on a part of the family history that I knew a great deal about—my own.

Along the way, I had help from many people. My neighbor Arlis Daily read early drafts of the work, making innumerable corrections to my grammar. My wife, Shaya, listened patiently to me as I reported to her my progress (or lack thereof) in writing the book. My brother, who is now deceased, spent hours with me on the phone recalling our childhood. John Reiger, a friend from graduate school days, encouraged me to pursue the project. Professor Steven Mintz of the University of Texas at Austin exchanged emails with me about the importance of producing childhood histories. And at a point where I had just about decided to abandon the project, I discovered Neal Samors' wonderful book, *Memories of Growing Up in Chicago*. My conversations with him gave me new life. Finally, the production staff at Bublish exceeded all my expectations in helping me turn the manuscript into a polished book. Of course, any errors in it are solely the responsibility of the author.

ABOUT THE AUTHOR

Charles Zucker was born in Chicago in 1945 at Ravenswood Hospital, where his mother, Leah, had been a registered nurse before retiring. He was raised in the Chatham-Avalon neighborhood on the city's South Side. Zucker graduated from Dixon Elementary School and attended Hirsch High School for one semester before the family moved to the suburb of Lincolnwood. After graduating from Niles Township West High School in 1962, he enrolled at the University of Wisconsin-Madison, where he majored in history, graduating in 1966. He then entered the PhD program at Northwestern University and received his PhD in American history in 1972. Zucker taught at Fayetteville (North Carolina) State University and at Carroll College (now Carroll University) in Waukesha, Wisconsin, before segueing into professional association work. In 2007, he retired after serving for nineteen years as the executive director of the Texas Faculty Association. He now resides in San Antonio, Texas, with his wife, Shaya. They spend their summers in Montana near Glacier National Park, where they enjoy hiking, fishing, kayaking, and the glorious beauty of the area.

Parts of this book have been reproduced from the author's previous book, *A Fisherman's Journey: A Lifetime of Angling Adventures from*

CHARLES ZUCKER

Northern Wisconsin to Northwest Montana, 1950-2020 (Sweetgrass Books, 2022).

Charles Zucker

Author's Brief Bibliography

Mintz, Steven. Huck's Raft: A History of American Childhood, Cambridge, Massachusetts, and London, England: The Belknap Press of Harvard University Press, 2004.

Samors Neal, with Thomas O'Gorman and Christopher Lynch. Memories of Growing up in Chicago: Recalling Life during the 20th Century, Troutdale, OR: Chicago's Books Press, an imprint of Chicago Neighborhoods, Inc., 2024.

Schaafsma, David, ed. et al. Growing Up Chicago, Evanston, Illinois: Northwestern University Press, 2022.

Streiker, Lowell D. The Old Neighborhood: A Chicago Childhood – 1942-1952. Troutdale, OR: 2006.

www.ingramcontent.com/pod-product-compliance
Lightning Source LLC
Chambersburg PA
CBHW060608080526
44585CB00013B/737